Purchasing for Manufacturing

Purchasing for Manufacturing

Harry E. Hough

Industrial Press Inc.
New York

Library of Congress Cataloging-in-Publication Data

Hough, Harry E.
 Purchasing for manufacturing / by Harry E. Hough. — 1st ed.
 224 p. 15.6 cm. X 23.5 cm.
 Includes bibliographical references and index.
 ISBN 0-8311-3066-0
 1. Industrial procurement—Management I. Title.
HD39.5H683 1996
658.7'2—dc20   95-25848
                                                            CIP

Industrial Press Inc.
200 Madison Avenue
New York, New York 10016-4078

First Edition

Purchasing for Manufacturing

Composition by Caryl Hudson Baron. Printed and bound by Quinn Woodbine, Woodbine, NJ.

10 9 8 7 6 5 4 3 2 1

Contents

Chapter 4: Why Good Specifications are Important, and How to Get Them

Chapter 5: Important Information About Iron, Steel, and the Industry

Acknowledgments

As a buyer and purchasing manager, I have met with hundreds of suppliers that sell the products discussed in this book. Some were only temporary sources for the products that I purchased, while others turned out to be long-time suppliers. Many invited me to tour their operations and were very hospitable during my visit. Undoubtedly, much of their attention had the purpose of obtaining business. In spite of those intentions, I cannot totally question their sincerity, for they were very helpful in providing an education to a sometimes ill-informed buyer. My thanks to them for helping me do a better job, and giving me information about buying their products to convey to other buyers and purchasing managers.

A special thanks is due to the members of the American Purchasing Society who also gave me the benefit of their buying experience and insights into the world of industrial purchasing.

Thanks to Hank Sauerman, formerly a buyer who reported to me and now Purchasing Manager of Seats, Inc., who provided me with updated information about the steel industry and steel purchasing practices today.

Thanks also to the many companies that allowed me to tour their facilities and answered my questions about their processes; in particular, Jason Redden, Jr., Michael McKee, and Michael Peppler, all of Coilplus-Illinois for their time and effort in showing me their modern service center. Thanks to James Courtney, Marketing Communications Director at Bethlehem Steel; Bert Delano, Director of Corporate Communications at Allegheny Ludlum; Mitch Haws, Director of Corporate Communications at Geneva Steel; Mark Tomasch, Senior Director Corporate Communications at the LTV Corporation; Robert J. Chidester, Manager, Corporate Communications at National Steel; and Don Mossgrove, Marketing Supervisor at

Weirton Steel Corporation. All of these individuals provided me with a stack of material to help prepare this book.

Special thanks go to Thomas Haring, Purchasing Manager of Tricon Industries, Incorporated, in Downers Grove, IL; and to Terry Drews, Materials Manager of Bellofram Corporation in Newell, WV; both gave me the benefit of their experience in buying castings and other products.

Thanks to all those companies who answered my written and telephone requests for information about their companies and their operations.

Finally, last but not least, thanks to my wife, Lynne, for her editing assistance and her support and understanding of the difficulties in completing this effort. Unequivocally, I accept full responsibility for any errors or omissions.

Harry E. Hough
January 1996, Port Richey, Florida

Purchasing for Manufacturing

CHAPTER 1

Introduction to Purchasing Operations

The Importance of Education and Experience

Some say that buying for industry is an art. Others claim that it requires many skills that must be learned both in the classroom and through on-the-job experience. Both viewpoints have merit. However, good buyers are not born. The skills required to be a successful buyer are necessarily obtained from both education and experience. The more education and experience you have, the better you are able to purchase products to meet the objectives of business.

Until recent years, there was very little written about how to buy or manage the purchasing function. There was even less written on how to buy specific products. Most of what was written were short articles that appeared in the various trade magazines. There are now plenty of books on how to negotiate. There are a fair number on how to buy and manage a purchasing department in general, but information about how to buy particular products is scarce.

If that is so, how have buyers learned the ins and outs of buying products for industry? Obviously, the answer is through experience. Years ago when I worked for Ford Motor Company, the policy was to rotate buyers so that they did not become too friendly with the salespeople. Another reason was to have them gain experience buying various products. Because of the frequency of changing buyers, salespeople used to half joke about the necessity of training new buyers. One may wonder what the cost of such

3

training was if the salespeople were really providing the information that the buyer needed to make a wise purchase.

Further evidence of the lack of buyer product knowledge is suggested from hiring methods. Interviewers either fail to ask potential candidates for purchasing positions about product knowledge, or say that product knowledge is not important. While it is true that fundamental capabilities are more important, if all other qualifications between the candidates are equal, the person hired should then be the one with some knowledge of the products that will be purchased.[1]

There are thousands of products that industrial purchasing managers are usually responsible to purchase—and they are expected to purchase each product wisely. Nevertheless, it would be impossible to have a thorough knowledge of every product. In spite of this, buyers buy these products and satisfy the needs of the organization without much trouble. The reason is in part because most of the items are of either low value or purchased in small quantities. Consequently, the correctness of every purchasing decision is not scrutinized closely. Also, high cost capital items are often shopped by the user who provides detailed specifications on the product that he or she wants.

Another (and perhaps more important) reason why most buyers stay out of trouble is because they use well-established purchasing techniques that limit the risk of buying. The early chapters of this book will discuss the normal purchasing system that helps buyers purchase the right products and services at a fair price and to have them delivered when needed. It is assumed that most professional buyers who read this book will know the fundamentals of buying, but these early chapters will be a good review of the essentials.[2] These chapters will also help those in other occupations who occasionally buy, and those who manage purchasing but do not normally get involved in the details of the buying function. Most of the rest of the book will then give the reader the information needed to buy specific products wisely.

Purchasing managers who have delegated the responsibility of buying certain products to buyers will find it helpful to read or skim the book in its entirety to get a general knowledge of each product. Buyers or managers who devote most of their time to buying these products should study the material so they will be fully familiar with the details.

Criteria for Selection of Products

The reader might wonder why certain products were selected for inclusion in this book. Products, or a category of products, were picked because they are commonly purchased by many industrial buyers in general, and by buyers for manufacturing companies in particular. Chapters on some products contain the names of suppliers of those products and information about the capabilities of those suppliers. While these names are in no way inclusive of all suppliers producing the respective products, they are representative and give the buyer a starting point for further shopping if necessary. The number and type of suppliers for other products is so great that it is left for the buyer to check the appropriate supplier directories for names and addresses. For a list of source directories, see the Appendix.

Information Needed to Buy Specific Products Wisely

Requestors for stock shelf items may provide a brand name or a simple description in place of a more detailed specification, but more is needed when buying either raw material or assemblies for production.[3] Some buyers of the latter simply refer to part numbers or stock numbers, but this is hardly considered informed buying by professionals. Intelligent buying means knowing how products are made: what research, labor, and materials go into the product. The buyer needs to consider whether the product is a "low tech" or "high tech" item; and whether the components of the product are easily obtainable or scarce.

The intelligent buyer wants to know about the industry that produces and sells the product purchased. Is it a highly competitive industry? How many sources of supply are available? While not impossible, certainly the ability to negotiate is limited if there is only one source or even if there are only a couple of sources. On the other hand, too many suppliers may mean that profit margins are so low that negotiating effort produces little results.

Use Purchasing Dynamics Methods

Many years ago, I discovered the importance of what I call "purchasing dynamics." In my mind, it is the idea that buying is a changing, active function. Unlike perhaps accounting—which basically deals with similar transactions and similar routines—purchasing requires imagination and action-oriented buying techniques. Less efficient and less effective purchasing operations use the same methods that have been used for decades. The buyers and managers in such departments waste time by attending to clerical functions. Their idea of purchasing is to wait for requestors to tell them what they need, and then to "place orders." They are order placers rather than buyers in the professional sense.

Those practicing purchasing dynamics are proactive. They don't wait for requestors to ask for material. They anticipate needs and begin shopping and negotiating for those needs. They develop automated systems and methods to reduce clerical work so they can devote more time to discussions with suppliers. They attend trade shows and visit supplier plants to learn about processes and new and better products. They don't blindly accept requests from users without suggesting better products or alternative ways of accomplishing the same thing.

Such buyers and managers work closely with their own marketing, engineering, quality, and plant personnel to gain their confidence and respect. They take part in establishing specifications that belong to their organization rather than to the supplier.

The old ways were inefficient and ineffective because time was used up on the clerical activities. Time was used to solve problems because of poor selection of suppliers, and less than satisfactory products were purchased. By automating and spending more time on selection of the proper source of supply and the proper product, time is saved for learning about new products and negotiating better agreements.

The Significant Profit Contribution of Good Purchasing

Companies do everything they can think of to boost sales revenue. Seldom are the owners and general managers satisfied to have sales remain static. Companies that are not too concerned about the amount of sales usually decline and eventually cease to exist. But too many times the concern about improving the sales figure is at the expense of other business functions. One of those functions—purchasing—may in fact indirectly provide more profit to the organization than can be obtained by raising revenue. It is now a cliché in purchasing management that it can take up to ten times or more in additional sales revenue to equal the profit of a 10 percent reduction in purchasing cost. The amount of profit generated by one additional sales dollar depends on the interest and the company involved, but it is not unusual for a company to only earn 5 percent on sales. Organizations sometimes only increase their losses by increasing sales. Out of every sales dollar, the cost of material, labor, and overhead must be deducted before there is any additional profit. But cost reductions by the purchasing function go directly into profit. If a buyer reduces the price of metal by 10 cents per pound, the company gains 10 cents toward profit contribution. If management would spend half the time on supporting purchasing efforts as they usually do in improving sales performance, the returns would be significantly greater.

The Organizational Structure of the Purchasing Function

Buyers in industrial purchasing departments, particularly in manufacturing companies, are usually classified as either MRO (maintenance, repair, and operating supplies), capital equipment, or production buyers (sometimes referred to as raw material). Depending on the size of the organization and type of organization, any individual buyer or purchasing agent may have responsibility for one or more of these categories. However, the reason for the distinction is that each category involves different buying techniques, and frequently different types of suppliers. The type of product category often requires dealing with different people within the buyer's organization. Service organizations such as banks, educational institutions, insurance companies, and government bodies buy many of the same items that fall under the MRO category, and of course buy capital equipment items as well. Because of their relatively low volume of purchases, the same person may handle both categories of items. This book focuses on production (or raw material) items, but many of the discussions can be applied to the other types of buying as well. The following may help clarify the differences.

MRO Buying

This category deals with maintenance, repair, and operating supplies. These items are frequently purchased in low volumes, sometimes as one or two pieces. Most of the time, the products have low unit value, although in the case of a repair item costing only a few pennies, a major job or even the entire plant may be shut down, costing many thousands of dollars. Some items, such as repair items, may only be purchased once and never again for the life of the machine using the part. A supplier may only be needed once for such items and never used again. Other items, such as paper towels, may be needed continually. MRO buyers are under pressure from many requestors to obtain goods or services quickly. Normally there is little planning involved by those requestors and many products are needed at once. MRO buyers may not be too concerned about the price of the product. Their primary objective is to satisfy the requestor. Purchasing managers realize that much of the cost involved with MRO is connected with placing and documenting the order. Thus, modern purchasing management looks for ways of reducing transaction cost such as use of EDI (electronic data interchange), system contracts, or so-called purchasing credit cards.[4]

Capital Equipment Buying

Items in this category may be physically very large. They may be purchased as a single unit, but multiple units may also be required. Although accounting may classify capital items differently for tax or financial purposes, the purchasing operation interprets them as those tangible items that have permanence, that are not consumable, that have a certain minimum dollar value, and that are used internally (rather than for resale). The purchasing operation may not even know or care how the accounting department classifies the item. It really doesn't matter, because the way accounting handles the charges does not affect how the purchasing structure or assignments are made.

For example, a calculator costing under $100 would certainly be assigned to the MRO buyer as an office supply and probably be expensed by accounting as well. A machine tool costing $50,000 would be considered a capital item by both purchasing and accounting. Accounting sets up capital items with an account to depreciate their cost over the expected life of the product. They are included as assets on the balance sheet. MRO items are expensed, that is, their cost is fully deducted at the time of purchase.

The same capital equipment item is so seldom purchased that known suppliers are infrequently used. New purchases of items used previously are reshopped, and new or untried suppliers are selected. Years may pass before buying a similar item again. During that time, suppliers go out of business or change their products.

Large capital expenditures frequently require more approvals in an organization. Although production buyers may have the authority to purchase many millions of dollars on their own signature, approval of a vice president, president, or board of directors may be necessary for a much smaller amount for a capital item. On the other hand, many companies have very loose control of the type of product that is purchased or the selection of the supplier. They are concerned about the amount to be spent but neglect to look at either the necessity for the purchase or the wisdom of the product selection. It is up to the purchasing manager to establish the proper controls.

Production or Raw Material Buying

The types of items in this category are used continuously by a manufacturing organization. They may be used in the manufacturing process without becoming an apparent integral part of the finished product for resale, or they may be a component of the finished product.

New purchases may involve different items even though the types of items are the same. For example, a job shop might order castings that are needed as a component for a custom product for a customer. If a company makes a proprietary product for resale, quantities of the same item may be purchased over and over for many years. Even in the automobile industry where models change their appearance every year, there are numerous parts that remain the same year after year. Consequently it is easy to stay with the same supplier, although it is not necessary. There are times when it is not wise to do so.

As in all buying, it is important to obtain delivery on schedule, to obtain proper quality, and to buy at the lowest cost. But these factors take on added importance when production quantities and schedules are involved. Because the volume of an item is high with production buying, it is normally relatively easier to negotiate a lower price than for MRO or capital equipment items. The same item could be purchased by different companies for different purposes. The company buying an item for production should be able to get a lower cost because of high volume. It should be stated, however, that there are reasons other than volume that may account for price differences. For example, a company may package a product for resale differently for the "after market" than it is packaged for production purposes. A part being sold as a repair item may have a beautiful four-color box. Inside the part may be wrapped in special paper and there may even be instructions included. The same item being sold for production use may be thrown loose into a large container and shipped in bulk.

Companies that sell items for production purposes sometimes refer to their customers as OEM (original equipment manufacturers) accounts. OEM prices can be substantially lower than prices given to others.

Purchasing managers for manufacturing companies spend the greatest percentage of time on raw material or production items. And well they should, for that is where the greatest percentage of dollars are spent. Careful analysis of production item costs along with enough shopping and good negotiating effort will minimize product cost. One reason that production items get so much attention is that keeping the cost low allows the finished product either to be sold at a lower price—and thus keep competition at bay—or permits the company to make a bigger profit. A combination of these usually results.

Manufacturing management may stress the importance of on-time delivery and that is very important. However, delivery problems may result from insufficient lead time or improper specifications rather than any deficiency either in purchasing or at the supplier. That is not to say that suppliers always do what they should or that purchasing follows up on orders as they should. I simply mean that the causes of delivery problems are as often in a company's own sales department, in scheduling, and in production control and inventory control as they are in purchasing or at the supplier.

Blaming purchasing for late deliveries fails to solve the problem and diverts purchasing from its profit producing function. This author believes that, on the average, the purchasing function can do more to improve a manufacturing company's profit picture than any other single department.

Let us look at the purchasing process before we discuss the methods of buying various products or product categories. The next chapter will cover the normal purchasing system and some important purchasing issues that affect all organizations.

Footnotes

[1] A high level of integrity checked by a thorough background investigation should be a must. Major qualifications should include good communications skills, a knowledge of negotiating methods, and the ability to use simple mathematics. Every applicant for purchasing should know some business law and be particularly familiar with the Uniform Commercial Code. Industrial buyers usually need to be able to read engineering drawings.

[2] For a full discussion of buying methods, see *Handbook of Buying and Purchasing Management* by Harry E. Hough and James M. Ashley, published by Prentice-Hall, 1992.

[3] Brand names should be avoided if possible. Sellers try to get their brands included on engineering drawings or included in other specifications provided by engineering or other requestors. Inclusion of brand names tends to tie the buyers' hands by excluding the competition and making it almost impossible to negotiate successfully. Sometimes a statement is included saying that a specific brand (or equivalent) is required. While this is somewhat better, very few products are exactly equivalent and the buyer is still restricted.

[4] Banks and credit card companies presently are using a high-impact marketing campaign to get businesses to use purchasing credit cards. The cards supposedly will reduce transaction costs, which on the average account for most of the MRO expense; but there is a serious question about proper control, and there are bank charges to the supplier which offset some of the savings obtained from reduced administrative cost.

CHAPTER 2

Essentials of Business Purchasing

Traditional purchasing methods for business are based on years of experience by thousands of organizations. Such experience shows that using certain methods helps minimize costs[1] and reduces an organization's risk. Normal purchasing activity involves the recognition of the need for a product or service, finding and evaluating the best qualified suppliers, obtaining bids, and negotiating a favorable cost. It involves the very important job of documenting the agreement to avoid misunderstandings or legal problems. Purchasing people are frequently further responsible to see that orders are followed or expedited to assure on-time delivery. They are responsible for resolving any problems connected with orders.

Determination of Need

In small or very loosely organized companies, someone may determine the need for a product and then go through all the steps necessary to make the purchase. However, in medium sized and large companies, as well as many small companies, the buyer is not normally the person determining the need for a product unless it is for use within the purchasing office. Buyers in retail organizations are the exception. They are more merchandisers than buying specialists. Retail buyers usually select the products to be purchased, are responsible for inventory and the sale of those products, and are responsible for the profitability of buying and selling those products; this is not so for the industrial buyer. The industrial buyer receives requisitions or requests from other employees within the same organization directing him or her to make purchases of particular products.

Evaluating the Request

Inexperienced buyers process the oral or written request without question. Usually the request is in the form of a written requisition. In recent years large companies, or those with well-developed computer systems, have been sending the request to the buyer through computer networks.

The experienced buyer will also process requests without too many questions if the items are regularly purchased, and if the quantities seem reasonable or if they are used in or by manufacturing. But new items, such as raw material or assemblies purchased for the first time or capital equipment items, require closer scrutiny. The professional buyer may question the wisdom of purchasing a higher grade of steel than needed, or the advisability of buying a tool which limits the quantity that can be produced to meet schedules. Such questions must be asked with great diplomacy and tact. The clever buyer can make profitable suggestions that the user may claim as his or her own idea, but eventually the buyer's value and contributions to the success of the organization will be realized and appreciated.

Finding and Evaluating a Source

An adequate purchase is only accomplished if the source is qualified and the need is legitimate. Then the buyer usually obtains the item without a problem, especially if the same item has been obtained many times from the same supplier and at the same price. However, if the item is new or if it is necessary to obtain a new or different supplier, a good buyer will ask a number of questions before placing the order. The type and quantity of questions depend on the company's policies, procedures, and organization. If the organization includes many qualified engineering departments, fewer questions about the design may be necessary. If the organization includes an elaborate budgeting approval and control system, fewer questions may be necessary about available funds and authorization of the purchase.

When a new buyer or purchasing manager arrives at a company that has been in business for many years, there are usually well-established sources of supply. The suppliers may have first sold to previous purchasing agents or they may have been introduced to the company by a secretary, a plant manager, or even the president of the organization. It really doesn't matter. The new buyer should evaluate those sources as if they were new and untried. That is not to say that previous performance records should be ignored. It simply means that in the competitive world of business, a supplier must constantly deliver a suitable product or service while meeting or exceeding what other suppliers may have to offer. At no time should a supplier be allowed to rest on past performance. Once an organization assumes it has the best sources of supply without considering what is available elsewhere, there is a strong likelihood that it will become uncompetitive in the marketplace.

Finding new or alternate qualified sources is usually deceptively easy. It is not uncommon for suppliers to be banging on the door to get a portion of the business that the buyer has to offer. Once in a while, the supplier of an item is hard to find. This sometimes happens with MRO items (maintenance, repair, and operating supplies), where a repair part is needed for an old piece of equipment. Buyers are sometimes frustrated when looking for an alternate source for a proprietary item. Buyers have asked me to help them locate an alternate source when a monopolistic supplier raises the price exorbitantly or when delivery or quality do not meet the standards desired by the buyer.

The methods are the same whether you are looking for a source to replace an existing source, or are obtaining a new item that you've never purchased before. Here are the ways you can find a source.

1. Check both general and specialized supplier directories.

2. Look at trade magazines for advertisements. In addition, such magazines sometimes publish the names and addresses of companies selling a particular category of product. Most industries have magazines that specialize in serving a particular industry. For the products discussed in this book, refer to the list of periodicals.

3. Attend trade shows. This is an excellent way of learning about new products and new sources of supply.

4. Contact industry and trade associations that frequently keep lists of members and their capabilities.

5. Get recommendations from other buyers and salespeople selling related noncompetitive products or services.

6. Contact the business or commercial section of foreign consulates.

They often have lists of companies and the products they make. The listed companies are interested in doing business in the United States.

7. Contact your professional purchasing association such as the American Purchasing Society. They have many reference volumes and are happy to help.

8. In-house files can be a valuable source of information if pamphlets, brochures, and catalogs have been filed and cross referenced. Some companies routinely throw out this material that has been sent in or dropped off by salespeople. It can accumulate and take up a lot of space. But if you have the space and time to maintain the files, it can be very helpful when you need it.

9. Even competitors may give you assistance. They realize that if they help you, you may be able to help them when they need assistance.

Even if the item has been previously purchased, the buyer should periodically obtain bids from other qualified suppliers. In either case, the buyer must find capable sources. It is not always easy to find the *best qualified sources*. Often nonpurchasing people underestimate how difficult and time consuming this aspect of buying is. The first step usually involves checking one or more of the multitude of source directories available. Nearly all libraries carry several directories of suppliers. Telephone books are useful to get a quick list of suppliers in a particular geographic area, but they provide little information about the companies listed. If an organization is located in a small town or rural area, telephone directories may be purchased for as many big cities as you wish. The price is modest but so is the information contained. The largest directory both in the number of volumes and the extent of its circulation is the *Thomas Register of American Manufacturers*. It consists of over a dozen large books with the names and addresses of suppliers listed in alphabetical order by products and services. A handier book that may be kept on a buyer's desk is *MacRae's Blue Book*. Neither of these directories gives much information about the companies, but they give enough information to establish contact with potential sources.

There are many other directories for specialized products, and many trade magazines periodically print lists of suppliers. (See the chapters on particular products, or see the Appendix for names and addresses of directories and periodicals.) It is a good idea to get subscriptions to all the trade magazines you can that pertain to the products that you are interested in. Subscriptions to most of these magazines are free to qualified buyers. Even if the magazines don't have a supplier directory issue, the advertisements are helpful when you are looking for a source. If you receive an issue that does contain a directory, make sure you save it for future reference.

The regular supplier directories are for sale. They vary in price between under $100 to over $600. Some of the directories give financial information such as dollar sales volume. Some give the number of employees, which is helpful in assessing a supplier's relative size.[2]

It is important to keep current directories available so that buyers can find sources easily and quickly. However, you don't need to invest in new editions of the same directory every year. Many buyers alternate between one directory and another from year to year. Thus they have a library of several different directories to choose from. Others send their older directories to other company locations that may not need to use them as frequently. For other considerations when selecting a source see Chapter 14.

Obtaining Bids and Prices

Once you have a list of potential sources, it is time to contact those sources to obtain bids. Buyers do this by telephone or by sending out Request for Quotation forms (RFQ). Most buyers prefer to telephone first to get some preliminary information or even a contact name before sending out a formal RFQ. It is not advisable to depend on the mails alone to get bids. Sending your request by FAX will probably get more attention and speed up an answer, although it may be impractical when many drawings or specifications need to be sent. If you use the mails, follow up with a telephone call to make sure the request was received and find out if there will be a response. The RFQ form or simply a letter may be attached to drawings or other specification sheets.

Making a request for a bid in the proper fashion is important to establish clear communications between the buyer and all potential sellers. Documenting all requests and information in writing avoids giving different information to different bidders. Except for the names and addresses of the supplier, exact copies of the bid request forms and letters should be sent to each bidder. Use forms that blank out the names and addresses of everyone other than the recipient so no suppliers will know whom they are bidding against. They may find out in spite of all efforts to the contrary, but if you can keep the names of the competition confidential, you are more likely to get a lower cost.

The major reason why a buyer is requesting a bid is not always clear to the supplier. He or she may be trying to find the lowest cost source in order to place an order. Sometimes cost information is needed for submission of budgets for approval. The department submitting the budget for approval may be including a wish list of items they would really like to have, but don't know for sure if the budget will be approved or don't know exactly what they want. Although such requests may be wasting a supplier's time, they have little choice in responding if they want a chance at possible business.

Often, the supplier has no way of knowing if the request is legitimate, i.e.,whether or not it is with the intention of really buying or just looking for information with little real chance of a purchase being made. Organizations should be careful not to abuse suppliers with such requests. A regular supplier who becomes aware of a cost burden connected with such requests may increase prices in order to cover the cost of making many bids without receiving corresponding orders. Other suppliers that never receive business may also increase prices or decline to bid altogether.

The request for quotation may describe the product that the buyer wants in general terms only so the seller may provide different specifications or different designs. In this case the buyer is not certain what he or she really wants. In other words, alternative designs may be better than what the buyer has in mind. This type of request may be initiated by engineers who are trying to define specifications, or it may be initiated by manufacturing people who are looking for different products that may do a certain job better or make it easier to make a product. Purchasing personnel may also initiate such a request, and it is good purchasing practice to do so in order to obtain the best products for the purpose intended.

Some requests for component or raw material price information are to help estimators establish a total internal cost to make the organization's own bid to give to potential customers.

Regardless of who initiates the requests, better purchasing objectives are achieved if all requests flow from the originator to the purchasing department. It should be a member of the purchasing department who contacts the supplier and requests information. If other department personnel deal directly with suppliers first, they may obtain bids that have little value because they are from unqualified sources, or that have unacceptable terms and conditions. Many a purchasing agent has been forced to make an uneconomical and unsatisfactory purchase because other department personnel have obtained bids and used those bids to establish firm budgets, or they have used up all the available time to look for qualified sources and negotiate a favorable agreement.

Analyzing the Bids

Picking the lowest cost supplier after the bids are received is not necessarily simple. You may not even receive answers from all the suppliers that you have asked to bid. There are various reasons for this, and you should attempt to find out why they did not bid, especially if you did not receive replies from several. For example, you may find that the supplier does not make or sell the product you asked for. Or you may find out that the supplier has no idle capacity and does not want to accept more business because he or she is uncertain about cost changes. Sometimes a supplier believes you are not serious about placing an order and that you are only fishing for information to use in bargaining with your existing sources who are his or her competitors. Sometimes you will find that your request has simply been misplaced or was lost in the mail.

If the supplier does not sell the product you wanted, he or she will often be able to tell you who does. Other reasons why a supplier did not submit a bid will let you know if you should try again in the future.

It is easier to analyze bids when each supplier is submitting prices on the same set of specifications. For this reason, better results can be obtained if time permits requests for quotations to be made in two stages. The first stage is used to gather information in order to prepare firm specifications. The second stage is used to ask for revised costs on the specific set of specifications you want. For example, as discussed later, there are various ways of making castings to provide different finishes. When you know what finish you want and what process will give you that finish, you can then be more specific about your requirements. Then, hopefully, each supplier will be bidding on the same things, and the analysis involves simply transferring the incremental costs from each supplier's document to a spreadsheet. In the past, this was done on a columnar sheet of paper. Many still find it easy to use the same method today, especially with uncomplicated purchases. However, if you are familiar with Lotus 1·2·3, Excel, or some other computer spreadsheet program, you probably will prefer to use it.

As indicated above, it is easier to analyze bids if you request firm bids based on clear and definite specifications. However, unless you insist on bids only matching those specifications, you may still get some variation. If you are involved in high precision work, government contracts, or items for the

military, such firm specifications are routine. In other cases, you are wise
not to be too insistent on your own specifications even at this stage. A supplier may not be able to produce exactly what you want or exactly the way
you want it. If the supplier's modification or revision is slight, it may be to
your advantage to look closely at the difference. Your spreadsheet should
then highlight the difference indicating that the specification is not the
same. To be fair to all the bidders, if the revised specification is seriously
considered, offer all other suppliers an opportunity to bid on the same revision, unless the revision contains some proprietary product or process.

A good and proper bid policy is one of the most important guidelines
that a purchasing department has. The policy should describe when bids are
necessary or required and how often they should be obtained. The antici-
pated dollar amount of the expenditure is used in determining if bids
should be required. Some policies base bid requirements on the accounting
category of the expected purchase. For example, it might say all capital
items require at least three valid bids. Many manufacturing companies
require that all new items used in production require bids. The majority of
policies require three bids, but three is just an arbitrary figure.[3]
Unfortunately, buyers are satisfied when they get three bids rather than
thinking it is a minimum. I believe a buyer should try to get as many bids as
time permits before reaching the point of diminishing returns. My experience is that an average of six bids is normally sufficient unless the expected
long-term expenditure will be very high.

It is recommended that bids be obtained periodically on items that are
continually purchased. The frequency depends on the value of the items
and the amount purchased. For production items, once a year is a common
target of purchasing management, but every two years is a more likely actual practice. It is a serious mistake to keep buying from the same source year
after year without checking the competition or shopping for a better offer,
regardless of how many suppliers originally bid or how uncompetitive they
were. Experience tells us that conditions change. New processes are devel-
oping all the time. Management and company philosophies change. New
suppliers come up with better ideas and better products.

Even if the present supplier is still the best choice, going out for bids
periodically keeps your present supplier alert and looking for ways to stay
competitive. It probably delays any impending price increase. It helps you
negotiate with a knowledge of the marketplace.

The bid policy should reflect how buyers should or should not negotiate with bidders. Government buyers are limited by regulations that sometimes prevent negotiating after bids are received, although even some gov-

ernment departments have liberalized their policy on this issue. Purchasing management should select one of these two policies: "First bid is the final bid" or "All bids are subject to negotiation." The reasoning of the first policy is to encourage suppliers to submit the lowest possible cost. This policy, so the theory goes, discourages use of inflated bids to allow for negotiation and later compromise. The disadvantage for the buyer is that nothing further can be done if no acceptable bids are received. When the second policy is used, the advantages and disadvantages are reversed. Suppliers are prone to inflate cost, allowing room for negotiation. However, the buyer has the advantage of negotiating before awarding any order.

Request for Quotation Forms often state one of these policies so the supplier is forewarned. More than a few buyers and purchasing managers prefer and use a modification of the above-mentioned policies. They omit any written statement to the supplier regarding the bid policy, and only disclose it if the supplier specifically asks. After the bids are received, they negotiate with the one or two lowest bidders.

Issuing Paperwork

The purchasing department of a business is one of the departments that uses many forms and generates a lot of paper. Because of the burden of handling so much paper, preparing the forms, distributing them to various people internally and to suppliers, and keeping files, efforts have been made to use different systems to minimize or eliminate such paperwork. While the intentions are good, it is a serious mistake to use inadequate documentation or to eliminate hard records of purchasing transactions. This is particularly true for manufacturing companies that spend a greater percentage of their revenue on purchased products and services than companies in the service industries.

Efforts to eliminate paperwork include the use of EDI (electronic data interchange), purchasing credit cards, blanket orders, traveling requisitions, and systems contracts. There are advantages and disadvantages involving the use of these devices. Generally, the older methods such as traveling requisitions, blanket orders, and systems contracts are more helpful in improving efficiency without weakening purchasing effectiveness.

EDI

Electronic Data Interchange, or EDI as it is usually called, involves sending information back and forth between buyer and seller to make purchases, send invoices, and make payment. Eventually, some form of EDI will probably be used for nearly all commercial transactions. However, various methods of data transmission to place orders have been used for over twenty years. They have not had wide acceptance because special equipment has been needed, and often different equipment or software is used by different buyers and sellers. Because of this nonstandardization, few buyers have been willing to lock themselves into a certain supplier because of the limitations of equipment or software. Today, the systems are more flexible, but still few organizations are using EDI to any significant extent, if at all.

Purchasing Credit Cards

Purchasing credit cards offered by American Express, Visa, and Mastercard for commercial transactions are being promoted to reduce transaction cost. Of course, the banks charge for the service, so each transaction incurs that added cost even though paperwork is reduced. The promoters point out the large cost involved in making each transaction. Those costs include the writing of a requisition, contacting the supplier, writing the purchase order, receiving the invoice, comparing the invoice and purchase order, issuing a check, and then filing all the documents connected with the purchase. By issuing credit cards to each employee, and allowing employees to contact the supplier and use the credit card to make the purchase, most of the paperwork can be eliminated.

The intended use of the credit cards is primarily for MRO items (Maintenance, Repair, and Operating supplies). Even so, there are purchasing executives who are reluctant to have them issued to nonpurchasing personnel. Instead, they give them to buyers to use. Other purchasing managers are comfortable giving them to nonpurchasing personnel, but restrict their use to purchasing approved suppliers, and to certain dollar limitations.

This author feels that the cards will weaken the purchasing function and be detrimental to the long-term interest of the organization. Purchasing people — to some extent — learn to resist selling pressure in order to make objective buying decisions. Nonpurchasing personnel often make unwise buying decisions and are more likely to do so if they are subject to sales pressure from suppliers. Furthermore, reduction in paperwork for MRO items can be accomplished by older and more reliable methods; these include the use of blanket orders, systems contracts, and the purchase order – purchase release method.

Traveling Requisitions

An old but effective system devised to reduce paperwork revolves around a form called a traveling requisition. The form is usually printed on heavy card stock so that it can be continually used without wearing out. Originally the form was developed for use by maintenance workers or for the person in charge of the storeroom or "crib." Each card is intended to record the purchasing information about one item only. The card shows the name of the supplier or suppliers as well as addresses and telephone numbers. There is a full description of the item. Each transaction is recorded along with the quantity, price, purchase order number, and date. The advantage of the form is that the user keeps the cards until it is time to reorder. He or she then fills in the quantity needed and sends it to the buyer. There is no need to look up anything, and there is no need to write much except the quantity needed and perhaps the date needed. When the buyer receives the card, he or she has all the information necessary to immediately place an order. Nothing needs to be looked up. A complete history of purchases of that item is at hand including the previous source, the usage over time, and the prices paid. As soon as the order is placed with the supplier, the form is returned to the user with the new purchase order number included and the scheduled delivery date.

The only minor disadvantage with the use of traveling requisitions is when they are lost or misplaced while moving from user to buyer or from buyer to user. This seldom occurs, and the disadvantage could be overcome by placing the form on-line in the computer.

Blanket Orders

Blanket orders not only reduce paperwork, they often reduce prices by getting volume order discounts. A blanket order is simply an order that covers requirements over an extended period of time. Usually they are issued for one year, but they may be issued for shorter or longer periods. The order may call for regular scheduled shipments, or may only indicate that the full quantity stated on the order will be purchased in the time stipulated. Buyers usually try to obtain firm prices, especially if the blanket order has been used to obtain a lower cost. However, if the primary purpose is to reduce the need to write many purchase orders, the price term sometimes is left open or is based on some preestablished formula. There are many varieties of blanket orders, and their use is only limited by your imagination. One caveat: if you are too vague, that is, if you leave quantities, prices, and schedules open, there may be no contract, and delivery of needed material may be in jeopardy.

Systems Contracts

You might think of systems contracts as extensions of the blanket order idea. They are used to buy many different MRO items that are often used by an organization and are usually purchased from industrial supply companies. Rather than go through the shopping and ordering process every time the items are requested, an agreement is made with a supplier to keep stock available to satisfy the requirements for any listed item. Requests for bids are sent to a number of potential suppliers and a contract is awarded to the supplier that has the lowest total cost for all items rather than for each item on the list. Prices are based on estimated usage and on the premise of obtaining all the business for the products involved for the duration of the agreement. Separate contracts with different suppliers may be given for electrical items, plumbing items, janitorial supplies, etc. The system saves an enormous amount of paperwork and buyer time.

In addition to paperwork reduction for small purchases, the purpose of any of these methods is to free up valuable buyer time to work on raw material and production item purchases where the much higher dollar expenditures are made.

Some companies have gone so far as to establish a policy of eliminating the use of purchase order forms without replacing them with any written document. Other companies produce purchase orders through the computer but fail to include either standard "boilerplate" or customized legal clauses that protect the organization's interest. This author believes that neither of these methods is worth the risk. That is not to say that purchasing operations cannot be streamlined to minimize paper handling by other methods. Use of blanket orders, traveling requisitions, systems contracts, and the computer can substantially reduce the number of hours needed to handle transactions.

Forms Used

The traditional, most frequently used purchasing forms are:

Requisitions

Requests for Quotations (or Requests for Bids)

Bills of Material

Bid Analysis Forms

Purchase Orders

Purchase Order Revisions

Purchase History

A description of these forms follows. In recent years, many companies have replaced some of these hard copies, particularly those used internally, with similar records kept in the computer or via communications through the computer.

Requisitions

The three major source documents that trigger buying efforts are the requisition, the traveling requisition, and the bill of material. Some larger companies use several different styles of requisition forms for different types of purchases. They may use a short form for incidental low cost items, and a longer, more detailed form for more significant purchases. Traveling requisitions were originally designed for use by either maintenance people or storeroom or "crib" attendants to order low-value MRO items used repeatedly. Companies have corrupted the intent of the traveling requisition by using it for production items and raw material that should be controlled more carefully than MRO items.

A requisition form with a good design includes the name of the requestor, the date the request is made, an adequate description of the item to be purchased, when the item will actually be needed, and the quantity needed. A space for an authorizing signature should be included.

It should be the responsibility of the user or supervisor of the user to prepare the requisition. Buyers and purchasing managers should not be required to prepare these documents unless they are responsible for determining the need as well as for buying the product. Rarely do businesses require buyers to prepare requisitions except in very small organizations.

Requests for Quotations

Many requests for purchase information — particularly prices, and often supplier capabilities — are made by telephone. However, professional purchasing people use a standard form whenever time permits or when high cost capital equipment or production items are involved. The RFQ form is a multipart form that includes spaces for supplier names and addresses, a space for a description of the item or items wanted, and spaces for other terms and conditions that the buyer wants, such as the desired delivery dates. Forms are designed so that multiple supplier names and addresses can be inserted, but only one supplier name and address appears on each copy. The copy received by the supplier only includes that supplier's own name and address, so the names of the competitive bidders are not disclosed. The cover sheet or first page may include a space for inserting and comparing bids next to the name of each supplier, although in most cases this space is insufficient and a bid analysis sheet must be used.

Bid Analysis Form

Although a standard columnar pad can be used, purchasing departments may use a form designed to compare the bids received. In recent years, more and more buyers are using Lotus 1·2·3, Excel, or some other spreadsheet program. They make analysis easier because as many rows or columns can be used as is necessary, and calculations can be done automatically once the formulas have been inserted. Corrections of mistakes are easier because all recalculations will then be done automatically as well.

Bill of Material

Frequently, the source document showing requirements for raw material, and especially component parts for manufacturing, is a bill of material. Sometimes the bill of material shows both items manufactured internally as well as items for outside purchase. In some companies, a production control or inventory control function will use the bill of material to transfer the actual quantities needed for purchase to a requisition form that is sent to purchasing. Computerization of production control, scheduling, and inventory control produces a document that is easier for purchasing to use. But the initial purchase of a production item should involve a requisition that includes more detail than is supplied by a bill of material.

Purchase Orders

It is no exaggeration to say that the purchase order is the most important form used by buyers. Nearly all businesses use some type of purchase order form. They come in all sizes. There may be as few as two pages or as many as twenty. The average is about five and has been decreasing over the past dozen or more years as purchasing departments have become more efficient. Here is the normal distribution that most companies use.

Original — to the supplier.

Acknowledgment copy (when used) — to the supplier.

Accounting copy — for internal use so accounting can compare invoices to the purchase agreement. In recent years, some companies have eliminated this copy and have used purchase information in the computer to make the comparison.

Receiving copy — for internal use so the receiving department can compare shipping documents to the purchase agreement. Some companies now have receiving personnel compare shipments to information in the computer. Computer terminals are located on the receiving dock.

Purchasing copy — an important copy to maintain safely with all supporting documents.

Other copies may include an extra copy for purchasing so cross-reference files may be kept in numerical sequence as well as alphabetically by supplier. Most companies have eliminated this duplicate by using the computer to index files by purchase order number as well as in alphabetical order. Some companies provide a copy to a follow-up person or expediter who makes sure delivery is made on schedule. Once in a while, you run across a company that gives a copy to the requisitioner. This is a poor practice because it circulates confidential information that may be disclosed to competitors, and therefore limits the buyer's negotiating ability.

If either hard copies of purchase orders are to be sent to receiving, or if information is provided by the computer that allows receiving to check shipments, then prices, terms, and conditions should be excluded.

Purchase order design is an often neglected area. It is a costly mistake not to take the time to design a form to allow purchasing to be as efficient as possible. A well-designed form minimizes typing or printing by including spaces and headings. The normally acceptable and most desirable standard terms and conditions commercially printed on the form will eliminate the need to type or print the same material on every new order. Commercial printing can reduce the size of the type so that it is still perfectly legible yet conserves space. Placing spaces for information in the proper order, i.e., as entered, reduces eye fatigue and speeds typing. An attractively designed form improves company image as well.

Using the computer allows buyers to select appropriate terms and conditions stored on disk. It eliminates the need to recompose terms for every new order, and helps insert well-thought-out properly composed clauses.

Purchase Order Revisions

Some companies use special forms called either purchase order revision forms or purchase order change notices. These forms provide check spaces to indicate the type of revision or change that is intended, and then spaces showing the old information and what it is to be changed to. For example, there may be a box to check for quantity change. Then there would be a space for the old quantity and another space for the new quantity. While this seems very elementary, it eliminates the need to type or redo the entire agreement if the change is acceptable to the supplier. The forms indicate that all other terms and conditions remain the same.

It is common practice to use purchase order forms to make changes, but this can be dangerous. When purchase order forms are used, the number may be crossed out and the original number inserted along with a revision number. However, preprinted terms and conditions on the form may create ambiguities if the original purchase order included different negotiated terms.

Purchase History

A purchase history is maintained when traveling requisitions are used; but companies that use traveling requisitions for MRO items usually use the normal requisition or bills of material for other items. Purchase histories of those transactions may be maintained on cards or in computer files. Recorded information includes the date of purchase, the name of the supplier, the price paid, the quantity ordered, and other information about the transaction. A history of bids received is valuable as well. All of this information is invaluable in estimating cost, planning purchases, and negotiating with suppliers.

A record of supplier performance is particularly valuable in order to make supplier evaluations fairly and objectively or to negotiate future purchases with a supplier.

Keeping Records

Purchasing records should be kept for many years. This is essential for legal protection and is also required by state and federal tax regulations. Retention of requisition forms is primarily for internal auditing purposes. Purchase orders and all supporting and related correspondence should be kept together in one file. Even sales brochures should be included if they describe the purchase product or the warranty, terms and conditions of sale, or any disclaimers. Handwritten notes about conversations or meetings should be kept with the file. Copies of certification of product or test results may also be included. All of this information will prove invaluable if there is ever any dispute about the product.

Any samples of material should be carefully marked with the name of the supplier, the purchase order number, and the date submitted. They should then be stored in a safe, protected area for reference if and when needed. Make sure samples are not mixed with regular stock.

Footnotes

[1] The word "cost" used in this context, and in most instances in this book, includes all cost associated with the purchase. Included (but not limited to) components of cost are price, transportation charges, payment terms, packaging, order processing, quality, scheduling, and risk factors.

[2] Buyers may obtain a free updated list of directories by writing to the American Purchasing Society, 11910 Oak Trail Way, Port Richey, FL 34668. Send your request for Buyers Checklist Number 1 on your company letterhead and include your name and title.

[3] A 1995 nationwide survey by the American Purchasing Society revealed that 4.5% of purchasing managers normally require two bids, 63.5% require three bids, 19% require four bids, 6% require five bids, and the remaining 7% require more than five bids.

CHAPTER 3

Negotiating and Keeping It Legal

All Transactions are Subject to Negotiations

In some ways, it is easier to negotiate for industrial products than other types of products; in other ways, it is more difficult. For example, negotiating with a retail chain store clerk is difficult, and finding the person in the store who will make price concessions is time consuming. On the other hand, consumers now have a set of laws and consumer protection groups who give them assistance when they get into trouble.

Salespeople calling on business and industry are more professional than most sales clerks, and understand the necessity of negotiating to obtain business. But industrial buyers are supposed to be professional, too, and therefore the consumer protection laws don't apply to them. It is *caveat emptor* (let the buyer beware) for them.

The principles and techniques of negotiating are no different for the consumer than they are for the professional business person. Today's buyer is more fortunate in having a wealth of information available describing negotiating methods. Twenty-five years ago, there was little or nothing available to help the buyer learn how to negotiate. There are now dozens of books that provide valuable guidance. We strongly recommend that every serious buyer should read several of these books. See the Bibliography for a list.

Once in a while a buyer will claim that you can't negotiate a certain product. In a seminar held by this author, one such buyer flatly claimed that no one gets a different price for steel. The buyer adamantly held this view in spite of the fact that other buyers in the meeting disagreed and tried to convince him otherwise. Most experienced buyers understand that all purchases are negotiable. What you can negotiate depends on your skill, your bargaining strength, and the methods you use.

Your skill can be developed by studying the available literature on negotiating techniques. Your bargaining strength is a function of the market for the item you want to buy, the flexibility of the seller, and your flexibility about the terms and conditions for an agreement. Let us look at each of these determinants of bargaining strength in more detail.

How the Market Determines How Much is Negotiable

It is said that negotiators are made, not born. Nevertheless, it helps to know a little economics and a little more psychology. During booms, it is more difficult to obtain concessions. When there is plenty of business to be had for the list price, why should a supplier reduce profit by cutting the price? When companies are busy filling orders, lead times are extended. It becomes more difficult to negotiate early delivery. When there are customers who are willing to pay as soon as delivery is made, it is more difficult to obtain extended payment terms. Note that we say more difficult, not impossible. You may be able to get what you want if you are a good customer or if you are willing to give up one thing for another.

Conversely, during slow periods negotiating becomes easier. When salespeople are clamoring for your business, you can obtain all kinds of concessions. However, smart salespeople don't let the buyer know that the time is right to make an advantageous purchase; the buyer must gather the information from his or her own sources and then use it to obtain a better deal.

The buyer needs to know what is going on in international trade, or in the nation, and in his or her own geographic area. The buyer needs to know what is going on in the steel industry, the casting industry, in automobile manufacturing, or in whatever industry affects the products that he or she wishes to purchase. For example, if you buy stampings and you are not in the automotive business, you still can be affected by how the automotive industry is doing. The automobile industry buys huge quantities of stampings, and when they are busy, many stamping companies are at full capacity. When automotive is slow, many stamping companies are then looking for customers.

Flexibility of the Seller

Some sellers will tell you right from the start that a price or terms of sale are nonnegotiable. Don't believe it. All things are negotiable. Whether you can obtain exactly what you want or get the seller to concede certain points is another matter. Obviously there are companies that are easier to deal with. There are those that will give in without much of an argument. Others will take a long time to give you the smallest concession.

The tough ones are a challenge. They require research to get as many facts as you can. They require planning, a well-thought-out strategy, and then skillful communication. Probably the most difficult part of negotiating with a hard bargainer is finding out what he really wants. That is not always apparent. In fact, it is seldom obvious. The novice will assume that price is the only major factor in a commercial transaction. Either side can obtain many other terms and conditions that will make price a secondary consideration.

Nevertheless, there are sellers who will not budge on price or other issues until you find out other items that are more appealing. By offering these other advantages, suddenly you may find the so-called nonnegotiable items can be discussed and then can be modified.

Flexibility of the Buyer

When you begin negotiating with a seller, it is wise to make a list of the items that you can give up and the items that you must have to make a deal. List the items in their degree of importance. Realize first that what is most important to you may be least important to the seller and vice versa. We all tend to assume that what is important to us is important to others. That is not always the case. For example, suppose you want delivery by the end of next month, and the price of the castings you need will be $1500 each. Your own salespeople insist that you must have delivery by then in order to satisfy the customer. The supplier claims their delivery cannot be made for 90 days. You are very unhappy about the price, but you are more unhappy about the delivery date. In the course of your discussions with the supplier, you get the supplier to say that the price can be cut to $1000 each, but 90-day delivery is the absolute best he can promise.

At this point, you are ecstatic about the price but feel that the delivery promise makes the lower price meaningless. Nevertheless, you describe the situation to your own salespeople. They say, "Hold on a minute. That lower price would increase our profits substantially. We will see if our customer will accept a 60-day delay." And so they ask the customer, only to find out that the customer — instead of being upset — is delighted. The customer was thinking about calling and asking for delayed delivery but was reluctant to spoil supplier relations. You may say this is far-fetched or an unlikely scenario, but I have experienced similar situations. Your particular case might be a little different, but the point is that what you might consider to be an inflexible issue is really not — if you can obtain other things that are more advantageous. It is the same for both buyer and seller.

Typical Commercial Terms

There are thousands of terms and conditions that are used in commercial transactions. Several dozen probably account for 90 percent of purchases. In addition to specifying the quantity and a description of the goods, nearly all transactions include terms that cover place of delivery, scheduled time for delivery, scheduled time for payment, method of payment, and the physical location where title to the goods passes from seller to buyer.

The buyer may specify the mode of transportation, but sometimes the seller has contractual arrangements with carriers or may have their own trucks that make deliveries. Selection of the carrier is a negotiable item.

The most common payment term in business is "Net 30," which means that payment is due within 30 days. The time for measuring when the 30 days begins is specified in the Uniform Commercial Code (UCC) Article 2, Part 3, Section 2-310(d) indicating that "...the credit period runs from the time of shipment but postdating the invoice or delaying its dispatch will correspondingly delay the starting of the credit period." However, if mutually agreed, terms can be different than stipulated by the UCC. A good negotiator may be able to obtain better terms. A poor negotiator may agree to less favorable terms. For example, a better payment term would be 2% 10, Net 30, which means that you can take 2 percent off of the invoice if you pay it within 10 days, but after that the full amount must be paid and it is due within 30 days. A less favorable term would be simply "Net," which means full payment when the invoice is rendered. The buyer and seller can agree on dozens of variations of these payment terms using fractional percentage discounts and extending the time limits. The good negotiator with a cash-rich company can trade good payment terms for price concessions. Conversely, the buyer may be willing to pay a little more to obtain extended payment terms.

The delivery-point-of-legal-possession term is especially important. That location is not necessarily where the final point of physical delivery of the goods will be made; it is the location where title to the goods passes from seller to buyer, and therefore the seller is no longer responsible for protection of the material. Consequently, neither is the seller responsible for the cost of storage or cost of transportation to the final destination. The usual term for domestic shipments is F.O.B. (meaning Free on Board) followed by the place where title passes. For example, F.O.B. Los Angeles would indicate that title passes from seller to buyer as soon as the goods reach Los Angeles. A more precise term would be F.O.B. buyer's plant in Los Angeles.

Two cost factors are involved in establishing the F.O.B. point: the transportation cost and the assumption of risk during transportation. If you obtain goods F.O.B. delivered, you have no risk until the goods are actually in your hands. If the goods are F.O.B. seller's plant, you assume all risks during transportation, and if something happens to the goods while on the way, you still have to pay for the goods even though you don't have them. You lose unless you have obtained insurance to cover any loss during transit.

Although you may be compensated for lost goods by insurance, there may be even greater cost if the material was needed for production and the supplier cannot replace it immediately.

Keep Transactions Legal and Avoid Costly Problems

Most transactions between businesses are concluded without legal problems. There are a percentage that cause small problems and sometimes very serious problems. Some are so serious that the organization is forced out of business, or employees and/or officers of the organization are fined or go to prison.

Unfortunately, most businesses operate without realizing the risk of legal problems, especially those caused by purchase of products or services or by the behavior of buyers and purchasing agents or other company employees affecting supplier activities.

There is an old saying that a little knowledge is a dangerous thing. Those who practice law amend that by saying that those who represent themselves are fools. Although I don't necessarily recommend representing yourself, nor do I suggest that you shouldn't obtain legal counsel for important busi-

ness matters — a little buyer education about the law helps prevent many of
the problems connected with purchasing.

Commercial transactions are interpreted differently than those made by
consumers. Business people are expected to know more about the law and
protect themselves accordingly. Consumers frequently can escape from contracts that they made hastily.

Buyers for business need to know a little bit about various law subjects.
There is no purchasing course in law school. The laws that affect purchasing
transactions fall under other subjects. For example, the law of agency deals
with who is empowered to conclude transactions on behalf of the organization. This is a very important topic for companies who want to avoid contractual responsibility for the purchase of items by unauthorized personnel.
If you allow employees to make purchases or order from a supplier, those
commitments may be enforceable even though those employees were not
authorized to make those purchases.

On the other hand, if a company delegates and authorizes a purchasing
agent to make purchases, it must honor the agreements that he or she
makes. The company cannot default on contracts by refusing to pay for the
goods without facing legal consequences.

What Every Buyer Must Know About Contract Law

Purchasing personnel should know the fundamentals of contract law.
Business people often fail to realize that buyers are making contracts when
they order goods. Contracts do not have to be in writing. In fact, contracts
can even be made without saying a word — that takes place all the time during an auction when a simple nod of the head is enough to make a binding
commitment. All it takes to make a legally enforceable contract is the following.

1. *Legal subject matter.* You can't make a legally enforceable contract to
   have someone murdered.

2. *Capable parties.* Parties who are insane or intoxicated can't make a
   legally binding contract.

3. *There has to be an offer and an acceptance.* One party must offer to sell or

do something for the other party. The other party must accept the offer. This area gets complicated because of interpretation of what constitutes an offer and what constitutes an acceptance. For example, taking delivery of goods and using them may indicate that the company has agreed to the terms of the transaction.

4. *There must be consideration.* Something must be given in return for something else. Usually money is given in return for goods, but some service or other benefit could be provided in place of the money.

Although it is not required that all contracts be in writing, lawyers and business people agree that it is important to have them written. It will be difficult later to prove what the terms and conditions of the contract or agreement were without a written document. The writings don't have to be in legal jargon or prepared by lawyers. Purchasing people routinely document contracts by issuing purchase orders. Salespeople use sales acknowledgements or sales order forms. The UCC (Uniform Commercial Code), which is now in effect in every state except Louisiana, requires that all contracts (agreements) for "goods" of $500 or more are in writing to be enforceable. "Goods" are tangible products as opposed to services. Before the UCC, there were disputes regarding contracts which were difficult to settle because of differences in laws and the interpretation of laws in different states. The UCC was recommended to the states and passed by the states to eliminate that problem. But the UCC only applies to goods. Agreements about services still fall under the older interpretations of contracts using the common law and judicial precedents. The purchase of both goods and services used to involve the "Battle of the Forms" which now only applies to the purchase of services.

The "Battle of the Forms" and the Uniform Commercial Code

What is referred to as the "Battle of the Forms" is caused by the need to establish when an offer is accepted. An offer in the form of either a bid or a purchase order (or by some action) may be accepted by sending an acknowledgement or accepting and using the product involved. Or the offer may be refused by making a counteroffer or communicating that the offer is not acceptable. Either buyer or seller can make offers or acceptances. For example, the buyer can make an offer by saying, "I will buy five cartons of your goods at the price of $100 each to be delivered tomorrow." Or the seller can say, "I will sell you five cartons of these widgets at $100 each to be delivered tomorrow." If the offer was made by the buyer, the seller can accept the offer by shipping the goods or acknowledging that he would ship the goods; if the seller did not like the $100 offer, he could make a counteroffer and say, "No, I won't accept your offer to buy at $100, but I will deliver what you ask for at $110 each." Often such a dialogue takes place through the use of sales order forms, purchase order forms, purchase order acknowledgement forms, and sales acknowledgement forms. Each side revises the terms of the form to suit its own wishes. It becomes almost comical as many offers and counteroffers about the same transaction are mailed back and forth. In some cases, goods are delivered and used while buyer and seller are still arguing over the terms of the agreement. The price is not the only issue.

To a large extent, this dialogue has been eliminated by the Uniform Commercial Code (or UCC) which states, in Article 2, Part 2, Section 2-207 (1) "...a written confirmation which is sent within a reasonable time operates as an acceptance even though it states terms additional to or different from those offered or agreed upon, unless acceptance is expressly made conditional on assent to the additional or different terms," and in (2) "The additional terms are to be construed as proposals for addition to the contract. Between merchants such terms become part of the contract unless: (a) the offer expressly limits acceptance to the terms of the offer; (b) they materially alter it; or (c) notification of objection to them has already been given or is given within a reasonable time after notice of them is received."

It further states in (3) "Conduct by both parties which recognizes the existence of a contract is sufficient to establish a contract for sale although the writings of the parties do not otherwise establish a contract. In such case the terms of the particular contract consist of those terms on which the writings of the parties agree, together with any supplementary terms incorporated under any other provision of this Act."

Know the Different Types of Warranties to Protect Your Interests

There are two types of warranties that buyers should be aware of: an express warranty, and an implied warranty. An express warranty is a warranty that is given by the seller either in writing or verbally by statements of fact or alleged fact. Those statements differ from simple sales talk that amount to bragging or exaggerated general claims of how good the product is. The law refers to those statements of opinion as "puffery." For example, a salesperson may say that his or her product is the best on the market; that does not constitute an express warranty. But if the same person says that the piece of equipment he or she is selling produces 1000 widgets an hour, then that becomes an express warranty, and the machine should produce 1000 pieces per hour.

An implied warranty is established when you buy from a merchant that normally sells a particular product for a particular purpose. The UCC states that an implied warranty of merchantability is given. The seller may avoid this warranty by telling the buyer that a product is not intended for the purpose the buyer wants and that it cannot be warranted for that purpose.

Any Business Buyer Can Violate the Antitrust Laws

The antitrust laws are complicated, and interpretation of them has varied over the years of their existence. Even well-trained corporate lawyers cannot always predict how the government will react to certain business activity. A general knowledge of what is flagrantly illegal will usually protect a business person. There is little chance that buyers will be found guilty of an antitrust violation if they use caution in what they say and do.

First of all, it is very important to realize that either or both buyers and sellers can be found guilty of antitrust laws. Second, if found guilty, the penalties can be severe. High fines and jail terms are possible.

It is illegal to conspire to fix prices or to conspire to restrict trade in interstate commerce. Don't assume that because you do business only locally that you are not involved in interstate commerce. The courts use a very broad interpretation of this aspect of the law, and most of the time it can be shown that your activity is involved in interstate business in one way or another.

It is illegal to discriminate in prices to curtail or to use your buying power to insist on a discriminatory price. For buyers, this is probably the most difficult and controversial aspect of the antitrust laws. How do you know you are asking for a lower price than others are paying? The answer is, you don't. Therefore, tread softly, watch what you say.

It is illegal to meet with other buyers in the same industry to force a supplier to reduce prices or to conspire with other buyers to boycott suppliers.

Reciprocity is illegal. In other words, you can't tell a supplier "we will buy from you if you buy from us." That doesn't mean that each company can't buy from the other. It only means you can't make one transaction dependent on the other.

Monopolies are not illegal, but monopolizing is. Although a violation is more than likely difficult to prove, buyers can recover damages from firms that use their power to restrict competition from entering the market.

Buyers Can Unknowingly Infringe
on Patent Rights

A patent is really a grant from the government for a monopoly for a period of time. If a buyer purchases an item that is patented from someone who has not been licensed to make or sell the patented item, the buyer can have the goods confiscated and may have to pay the patent holder for damages. For example, if the buyer purchased a component that infringed on some patent, the goods purchased would have to be surrendered or destroyed, and any profit made from the sale of those goods would have to be given up. Buyers can protect themselves somewhat by making sure there is a clause in the purchase agreement that guarantees the delivered goods will not infringe on any patents.

CHAPTER 4

Why Good Specifications are Important, and How to Get Them

It can almost be said that good specifications are essential for good purchasing. Specifications are really nothing more than detailed descriptions of a product or service. Sometimes they include drawings or sketches. For complex or technical items, particularly for manufacturing, those drawings were previously referred to as blueprints because of the blue colored paper or blue lines used. Now they are more commonly called engineering drawings because the drafting department usually is supervised by engineering.

A well-qualified buyer should, to some extent, be able to read and interpret the drawings, regardless of wherever they were prepared or whoever prepared them. A minimum knowledge of how to read drawings and the symbols used is very helpful in working with suppliers and working with engineers and others in the organization. The buyer may even be able to see deficiencies in the drawings and point out obvious errors.

Some buyers who are not technically trained are intimidated by engineers and other technical people because they do not feel they have the knowledge to question specifications. That attitude is sometimes encouraged by insecure, incompetent, or jealous technicians or engineers. You might say it is the "don't step on my turf" syndrome. But the buyer may be held responsible if the supplier does not produce proper goods or if costs exceed budgets.

There are many examples of improper specifications issued by major corporations. Engineering departments under pressure to reduce overhead may not do all the things that are necessary to protect the company's interest in the long run. Following are some real-world examples of actual improper, inadequate, or inappropriate specifications that seriously hurt performance.

A vice president of engineering for a major U.S. housewares company was adamant in refusing to provide drawings of proprietary components. He said he did not have the staff to do so and was not willing to spend the money to hire engineers and draftsmen. He insisted that the supplier do the design work and prepare the products from oral descriptions of what was needed. As a result, the buyer was "locked in" to the original supplier and was forced to accept exorbitant price increases. Competitors of the company that were not so restricted were able to make large inroads into the market and almost caused the company to go bankrupt.

For many years, the engineering department of a major capital equipment manufacturer issued drawings without approval signatures, without proper dates, and without revision numbers. No updated file was kept of drawings, and it was often impossible to even locate a drawing for an item currently being produced by a supplier. Consequently, the quality control department had great difficulty comparing delivered goods to the proper standard. When purchasing ordered the same item from two or more suppliers in order to meet delivery schedules, the new supplier sometimes received an out-of-date drawing. Supposedly, the same items received from different suppliers did not match and could not be used with other components.

An engineer with one of the "big three" automobile manufacturers gave oral instructions to a supplier to make changes in an item that was previously contracted and documented by a purchase order with the original design without the change. Purchasing was not notified of the revision and thus no paperwork was issued documenting the modification. The change resulted in an added cost of several hundred thousand dollars. The supplier billed the company, but the company refused to pay for the change. Settlement was made out of court, but the damage to the reputation of the engineer and supplier relations was difficult to correct, not to mention the added expense of the change.

The Importance of Knowing the Intended Use of Products Before Purchase

The buyer should know what a product is going to be used for. This will help him or her shop for the best product for the purpose. It will help the buyer communicate effectively with the supplier. It will help the buyer negotiate the best purchase. Engineers and even buyers have been overheard saying that it is none of the supplier's business what is done with the product. However, in nearly all cases, it is advantageous for the buying company that the supplier knows the intended purpose of the product. It has a double benefit. 1) It helps the supplier make recommendations on specifications that may be better than those prepared by the buying company (after all, who should know the product better than those who make it?). 2) A seller is legally responsible to advise you if the product you ask for will not do the job as long as the supplier knows your intended use. You, as buyer, still have the option to override the seller's advice, but as a merchant of a product, the seller should know what it will or will not do.

Preparing Engineering Drawings and Other Written Specifications

In most cases, drawings and specifications are prepared by engineering so the product can be either made or purchased to those specifications. Well-qualified engineering departments usually do most, if not all, of the work themselves. Nevertheless, not infrequently, suppliers are asked to submit bids or provide product information. In some cases, various departments need to obtain price information in order to prepare budgets for approval to purchase in the next year or sometime in the future. When information or preliminary bids are being obtained, great care must be taken to prevent being locked into a certain source, particularly for long periods of time, and especially if any significant amount of time has elapsed between the submission of such information and the time the order is placed. What may have been the most competitive supplier when the information was obtained many months ago, may no longer be so when you are ready to place the order.

When it comes time to place the order, no buyer should tell the supplier the amount that is in the budget until after a firm offer has been received. Only then may it be revealed as a negotiating tactic if the supplier's bid was more than the budget. It can then give the supplier an opportunity to match the lower budget figure. Many times, suppliers are able to reduce the buyer's costs by reducing the price or changing the design to meet budget limitations. But it is unlikely suppliers will offer to make design changes unless there is some motivation to do so.

Standard and Nonstandard Written Specifications

Typed or printed specifications are often attached to purchase orders. These written requirements may be supplied by various user departments or various engineering functions. For example, when this author worked at Ford Motor Company, we had both extensive written specifications as well as drawings. Many other companies provide suppliers with details of the required chemistry of raw material or products used in the manufacture of finished products.

There are two types of standard specifications. One refers to those specifications developed by an organization for its own use, but which are standard purchasing requirements for many products purchased from any number of suppliers. Standard printed specifications for processes and materials that are repeatedly purchased or shopped eliminate much typing and proofreading. Time is saved by having the standard specification forms available to give to suppliers or potential suppliers.

The other type of standard specifications are those made by various outside associations or organizations. Here are examples of some of the most common specifying bodies and their abbreviations.

AISI	American Iron & Steel Institute
ASME	American Society of Mechanical Engineers
ASTM	American Society for Testing and Materials
CSA	Canadian Standards Association
FAR	Federal Acquisition Regulation
ISO	International Organization for Standardization
MIL	U.S. Military
SAE	Society of Automotive Engineers
UL	Underwriters' Laboratories

Preparation of Drawings

Drawings of products are most often provided by the buying organization to suppliers for custom designed items. The drawings may be prepared manually by draftsmen or engineers employed by the buying organization. There is no reason why buyers or other people in the organization cannot supply simple drawings except that the buyer may have to accept the products produced even if they don't do the job that was intended. However, sometimes manufacturing people with little training provide simple drawings that may be sufficient. Someone with an idea may sketch a design on a napkin or scrap piece of paper. Although valuable items have been produced from such simple communication, it is not the way that buying is usually accomplished successfully. Delivering quick and carelessly made drawings to a supplier can result in costly mistakes. Delays until the directions are clarified are to be expected. The buyer should try to take the time to review such drawings for obvious errors.

Today, companies are moving from manually prepared drawings to computer generated drawings (CAD, or Computer Aided Design). Inexpensive computer programs are available that help the designer, engineer, or draftsman prepare drawings easily and quickly.

There are certain standards for drawing preparation. Those standards involve the use of specific symbols, and different symbols and styles of drawing are appropriate for different industries. For example, mechanical drawings, architectural drawings, and drawings for electrical or electronic products are quite different. Architectural drawings are used for construction work and include floor plans or layouts of buildings. Mechanical drawings are for machinery, assemblies, and components for manufacturing.

An assembly drawing is a representation of what the item looks like when complete, but it is nothing like a photograph. It may show features hidden to the eye by use of special broken lines, patterns of lines, and shading. Assembly drawings may be accompanied by detailed drawings of components of the assembly. Drawings may be supplied showing steps in the production process. For example, there may be a drawing of a component showing a rough configuration of a casting or forging before that item is machined to its finished size or shape.

Common and Essential Drawing Items

There are certain items that are common to all drawings and should be included for proper communication. It is far better to use industry standards than devise symbols and drawing styles unique to a single organization. Here are some things that should be included on every specification drawing.

Standard Symbols: Use wherever possible to avoid confusion or misunderstanding.

Title Block: An area of the drawing, usually in the lower right-hand corner, that indicates a name for the item shown, the name of the organization preparing the drawing, the name of the draftsman and/or engineer approving the drawing, the date the drawing was prepared, the revision date (if any), and the drawing number. The scale and units of measure of the drawing are usually included in the title block.

Sufficient Views: Every drawing should have a sufficient number of views to convey a complete understanding of the design of the finished product. An isometric drawing is a single view that gives a general idea of the finished product but is usually insufficient to adequately describe the item. Normally three views are required for most items: front, top, and side. Sometimes two views are enough if the product is symmetrical; and other times more than three views are necessary to adequately show complex shapes and configurations that are hidden in other views. Additional views or added drawing sheets may be used to provide detail that would be confusing in a larger view. Dotted lines normally illustrate hidden areas, but they are not always sufficient to show what is intended.

Dimensions: Drawings should have enough dimensions to assure little doubt about the size of the item or any of the item's areas. Those dimensions include radii or diameters as well as straight edges or sides. Draftsmen often will minimize the number of dimensions to avoid confusion or clutter. They assume that certain dimensions can be calculated from other dimensions, but it is better to duplicate a dimension than not having a way of figuring out what is intended.

Tolerances: No measurement is totally exact. Measurements are only accurate to a certain maximum or minimum amount. The difference between the theoretical measurement and the actual measurement is called a tolerance. Allowable tolerances should be clearly indicated in all areas of the drawing. For example, there should be a default tolerance that may appear in the title block; but if another allowable tolerance is needed for a hole or some area of the drawing, it should be clearly marked. Tolerances may be given in fractions or decimals such as: 6" + 0.005 or -0.005 (read: six inches plus or minus five-thousandths).

Material: If the drawing is for an item that is completely homogeneous, the type of material used may be shown in the title block. For example, it may show 1013 steel being required. If the drawing is an assembly, a separate materials list is often included on the drawing. In addition to the type of material, the quantity is sometimes shown. For example, 8 pcs. 1/4" X 3" galvanized screws. The list of materials may appear in the upper-right, upper-left, or elsewhere on the drawing.

Written Verbal Specifications

Some items need not, or cannot, be described by using drawings. Commodities and bulk raw materials need to be described verbally. That does not mean that such descriptions must be vague. They may be quantified and qualified as well as any drawing that illustrates the geometric shape of a product. Such items would include chemicals and standard raw material. For example, sulfuric acid could be specified by indicating its concentration and other details such as how it is to be packaged. Standard sizes of metal purchased from mills or warehouse distributors do not require drawings. A verbal description is sufficient.

Avoid Brand Names

Although it is sometimes necessary (for reasons of economy), the use of brand names should be avoided on all specifications. Sellers are eager to get their brands included on drawings or specifications but, in most cases, the use of brand names prevents buyers from obtaining the lowest cost and usually delays changing sources when that is necessary.

Engineers and others sometimes use brand names to hope for a certain standard of quality associated with advertised and recognized brand names. However, standards of quality often change with changes in company ownership or company management. It is better to use your own specifications or industry-wide specifications rather than accept a vague specification provided by use of a brand name.

Sometimes the brand name is specified with the addition of the phrase "or equivalent to." While this is somewhat better than using the brand name alone, it still is of dubious value. Few things are 100% equal. Arguments result in the interpretation of what is or is not equal. Slight variations in product specifications from one supplier to another may not really be very important. Nevertheless, the cost differential between two products may be significant. Even purchasers of consumer products for the home realize that the majority of lower priced generic products are identical to more expensive brand products that are widely advertised.

The Importance of Keeping Old Drawings and Other Specifications

All purchase orders or other contract documentation should reference the applicable specification in the description of the product. The date of the original specification or drawing as well as the drawing number should be indicated. If it is a revised drawing, the date of the revision and the revision number should be used.

Copies of engineering drawings and other specifications should be kept even though they may be obsolete or may have been revised. Such information is important in disputes over contracts or cases of liability for accidents. These old files are important to ascertain who produced certain components and at what period they were produced. They help determine what matching parts or components were needed at that engineering level.

Infrequently, more than one supplier produces an item for the same use, but with a slightly different design that does not affect the performance of the item. It is important to mark all documents with the specification that is appropriate for that design; and, in fact, a deliberate plan to give different suppliers slightly different designs is a good idea. It will pinpoint responsibility and avoid arguments about who delivered the items. The difference in design can be as simple as an embossed letter or number that would indicate who supplied that particular piece. Castings frequently carry a mark that indicates which casting supplier made the item.

Marking Drawings for Restricted Use— Proprietary

Drawings or other specifications designed or prepared by the buying company should be clearly and conspicuously marked that they are confidential and the property of the buying company (by name), and that they are not to be shown or the information contained should not be disclosed to anyone not connected with the supplier's internal operation. A stamp may be used, or the necessary wording may be printed directly on the drawing or specification forms.

A large engineering investment is involved in the preparation of drawings and specifications, and such information should not be treated lightly. Some suppliers will use one customer's information to help another customer or even to produce the same items for another customer. Some companies will go to great lengths to obtain proprietary information. For example, this author witnessed a flagrant case of industrial espionage while visiting a national tooling trade show. One of the machines on exhibit was a large multioperation tool about 50 feet long. A person posing as an interested potential customer asked if he could see the drawings. The very large drawings were brought out and spread across the floor of the exhibit area. At that point, an accomplice appeared with a camera and—before anyone could react—snapped pictures of the drawings and then ran off with the salespeople in hot pursuit. Meanwhile, the "potential customer" took the opportunity to disappear. Neither man was caught. Not many months later, a similar machine with a much lower price was introduced into the market from an international source. The foreign supplier was able to offer a much lower price because of lower development cost and because of lower labor cost in the country of origin. The domestic manufacturer had some very difficult financial conditions for several years thereafter.

Allowing the Supplier to Make the Drawing or Specification

Although it is better for the purchasing company to prepare its own drawings and specifications, it is not always practical. It may be uneconomical because of the low volume of product needed, or because internal engineers and technicians simply do not have the qualifications to do the job properly.

Companies often will make some of the drawings and/or some of the specifications and leave the details to suppliers. For example, a company may produce a drawing of a part that will be machined from a casting or forging, but will leave the specification details of the raw casting or forging to the subcontractor. Drawings for patterns may be produced by the supplier or subcontractor as well. The buying company may have all the skills necessary to produce the finished product, but the better qualified people for the raw material requirements are employed by the supplier.

Nevertheless, the buyer should try to obtain as much information about the raw material specifications as possible. Usually engineers for the buying company will at least want to discuss the specifications for the raw material with the supplier, and it is wise to obtain written documentation where possible.

The Importance of Obtaining Copies of Supplier Drawings and Specifications

Although suppliers may be reluctant to provide specifications or drawings to the buying company, it is important to insist on receiving those drawings. Suppliers like to avoid supplying such information so the buyer cannot obtain competitive quotations or resource to another supplier, but the buyer should have that prerogative, and the drawings may be needed for various other purposes long after the supplier has vanished.

Suppliers sometimes offer the excuse that a set of drawings is expensive to produce. It is usually worthwhile to pay for the drawings if that is the only way you can obtain them.

Another excuse is that there are no formal drawings. Beware: either the supplier may not be telling the truth, or the supplier may not provide consistent product without clearly defined specifications.

Reference to Drawings and Specifications on RFQ's and PO's

Any buyer has to be careful when asking for bids, especially by the use of formal Requests for Quotations. It is very helpful to use such forms to obtain similar bids, that is, bids for the same type of material. You will then be able to measure or compare the bids more or less easily so that you will be comparing "apples to apples." Nevertheless, you have to be alert to any differences not only in the prices, terms, and conditions, or legal boilerplate, but to minor differences in the material specifications. Although you may clearly state that you want a bid on a particular type of material, for example, a steel made with certain chemistry, the supplier may not submit a bid for exactly that type of material. Although it may be rare, this is sometimes done so that the supplier is able to submit a lower bid than the competition. More often, other material is substituted because it is the usual product made by the supplier or because the supplier does not have the immediate capability to fulfill your precise request. Usually the salesperson will point out the differences, but not always. A slight difference may not affect your operation; however, it may cause many problems such as mixing different materials and making testing difficult, or the material may not perform as intended.

Busy buyers with minimal clerical help may get into the habit of using a very brief description of the material on a purchase order and then simply refer to the bid or quote form submitted by the supplier. This can become a dangerous habit. If the material specified on the supplier's bid form is different than what you requested in your RFQ, too bad. You have just changed what you asked for and made a contract for the supplier's specification. In addition to possible changes in the product, by referring to the supplier's bid, you may have either accepted the supplier's terms and conditions in their entirety, or because of conflicts or ambiguities between your purchase order terms and conditions and those on the bid, you have left the interpretation of the intended agreement for the judge to decide. In other words, in one place on the form, you state the purchase shall be thus and thus, and in another you state the purchase is for the offer made by the supplier. If you later have a dispute and a judge must decide who wins the case, the contradictory terms will be thrown out and the judge will make the decision on what was meant or appropriate.

Authorizing Supplier Changes

Once a supplier is established as the source for components such as forgings, castings, or even assemblies, the buyer must be very careful when considering changing sources. Likewise, engineers or users must be careful not to tell a supplier to make changes in a product's design or even change quantities being produced without discussion and agreement from the buyer.

Generally, it is important that all part revision information be delivered to suppliers by the buyer, and all sourcing decisions be made by the buyer after discussion with engineers and users. This will avoid misunderstandings and will prevent problems with mismatched inventory, overstocks, shortages, and broken contracts with suppliers.

Measuring, Testing, and Certification

Purchased goods may be tested at the supplier's plant during manufacturing or after completion. It is also common for the buying company to inspect and test items after receipt. Sometimes, especially in small companies, the receiving clerks are the only people that do the inspection and testing. This may be completely satisfactory for low tech items or items that do not require close tolerances or critical requirements, but it is usually not sufficient otherwise. Receiving clerks seldom have the time to do more than superficial checks. They normally look for obvious flaws, make sure the quantities are correct, and that the general description of the product matches the documents.

Quality assurance by the buying organization and during manufacturing at the suppliers is usually carried out by a quality specialist. Likewise, received items requiring close quality control are most often checked by a quality function rather than only by a receiving clerk.

Providing specifications that show how products will be measured or tested helps both the supplier and the internal inspector. A quality control or quality assurance function often prepares such specifications and gives them to the purchasing function to pass along to the supplier with the purchase order or other documentation of the agreement. Such specifications are most important for items requiring close attention.

Specifications and Supplier Certification

There are different ways to help give assurance that products will meet the buyer's requirements. The obvious way is to provide a detailed description and sometimes technical description of what you want delivered. But, indirectly, you can help achieve better quality and have more confidence in the products you buy by making sure you have well-qualified suppliers. One way of doing so is to evaluate the supplier's capabilities before you order as well as during the period of the transaction. Purchasers for business frequently maintain a list of approved suppliers—these are suppliers that have been evaluated one way or another. Those evaluations take the form of reference checks, physical inspection of the supplier's facilities, and an evaluation of a supplier's policies and procedures. Particular attention may be given to the supplier's quality control system and facilities.

Individual companies have been doing these types of evaluations for many years. For over 20 years, the American Purchasing Society has advocated the establishment of third-party evaluations that would reduce the cost to the buyer and establish reliable and impartial standards for industry. More recently, that idea has gained support through the efforts of the International Organization for Standardization (ISO), a worldwide federation of national standards bodies.

ISO certifies that an organization has met certain standards. In other words, they use established and documented policies and procedures. European companies insist that the companies they buy from have been ISO certified. Now American companies are doing so also—particularly those companies who wish to do business in Europe or elsewhere outside of the

United States. While those companies who attain such certification have met a worthwhile standard, that alone is insufficient grounds for making a sourcing decision or documenting requirements for any product. Supplier certification is of value. Product specifications are still needed. The buyer should also be careful not to exclude very capable suppliers who have not applied for ISO certification.

Use Value Analysis to Improve Specifications

Value Analysis (VA) is a systemized way of studying a product or service to maintain or improve its function at a lower cost. Traditionally, VA is conducted by committees made up of representatives from various departments within the organization. The representative need not have any technical knowledge since in the initial stages no idea is discarded, regardless of how outlandish. In fact, the brainstorming sessions encourage "outlandish" suggestions. Often technical people fail to consider certain methods because they believe them to be impractical. But new ideas with some practical revisions often result in new and better ways of doing something.

VA involves accurately defining the function that the product serves, brainstorming for alternative ways of performing the same task, evaluating the cost of those alternatives, and then implementing the lowest cost alternative. For example, it might be less expensive to produce a certain part from a casting rather than use two or more stamped parts that are fastened together. Or it might be less expensive to use a forging in place of a casting to reduce rejections or reduce machining time.

The use of VA in the aircraft industry goes back 50 years. Since that time, major corporations have given courses to their buyers and engineers to encourage the use of VA (or Value Engineering as it is sometimes called). I attended a course given for Rockwell employees in Detroit back in 1971. Later I was on the VA committee at A.B.Dick Company in Chicago. In both cases, very significant cost reductions were achieved. Yet, eventually, the programs foundered because of organization restructuring at those companies.

Nearly everyone who knows anything about VA will agree that it is a very worthwhile method to reduce cost. In spite of that, few companies other than the "Fortune 500" use it on a regular basis. Part of the problem is that, while the merits of the system are recognized at lower levels of the organization, chief executives may not realize the advantages. Even if they do, they do not allow for the time required to do the work.

Members of the VA team usually have other jobs. They attend the VA meetings once a week or once a month and then go back to their respective jobs. Thus, little of their time in the VA effort is measured or planned for in the company budget. With downsizing of organizations, staff positions and administrative areas including purchasing often are those affected first and those are the areas that normally provide the people who make up the Value Analysis committee.

One of the key members on the VA team is someone from purchasing. Purchasing often takes the lead in establishing and continuing VA programs. This is because purchasing probably has as much if not more to do with the favorable results from VA efforts. Even when engineers agree to make a change in an internally manufactured item, the change may result in different purchased material or different purchased quantities of material. More often still, the change may involve changing suppliers or requiring suppliers to change the specifications on the items they supply.

Buyer Analysis

Whether a company has a formal Value Analysis committee or not, a well-qualified buyer can perform a similar task alone. The average buyer, for the most part, accepts the initial design from engineering even though suggestions can be made to improve the product's specification. If the buyer is given sufficient time to get involved in the total product design, the buyer can provide valuable input regarding the availability of material and the relative price advantages of different types of material. For example, the buyer may not feel there is a casting source that can provide a given piece with the desired quality level.

But, in most cases, the buyer accepts the initial design and begins to shop and negotiate for the best source for that design. Only if the buyer has difficulty getting a source to make the item as specified, or has difficulty obtaining a target price, is he or she likely to think about alternative designs. The buyer assumes that engineering has provided the optimum design. Frequently, companies permit or encourage engineers to discuss the design with various suppliers. Thus, the engineer evaluates the type of material or other specification based on what information was received from suppliers. If this was done objectively, with accurate information and with engineering analysis, the design may indeed be optimum. However, sales effort by the supplier combined with either an overloaded engineering staff or an unqualified engineering staff may result in a design that works, but that is needlessly expensive.

The solution to the problem is to plan enough time for buyer and engineer to work together with one or more suppliers to obtain an optimum design and specifications.

CHAPTER 5

Important Information About Iron, Steel, and the Industry

Learn as much as you can about the products you buy, and continue to learn as long as you are involved in their purchase. It will either keep you ahead of, or on a par with, the salespeople you deal with. Those salespeople spend all their time learning about the products they sell. The more you know, the better your purchase will be. If you buy iron or steel (or iron *and* steel) products, there is a lot to know.

What Steel Is and Where It Comes From

Steel is one of the most widely used products in the world. To a large extent, the amount of steel used in a society determines how we view the level of that society's advancement (at least that used to be the case not too many years ago). Steel is essential for the way of life in civilized countries.

Steel is used in the tools and machinery that make thousands of products. It is what many thousands of more products are made of. Bridges and buildings are made of steel. Automobiles, ships, and trains are made of steel. Tiny fasteners are made of steel. Household utensils and appliances are made of steel.

Yet steel itself has to be made before it can be used in other products. It is not made of one element. It doesn't come directly out of the ground. Nor is all steel the same or made of the same materials. It comes in many varieties. There are relatively soft steels and very hard steels. There are stainless steels that resist rust and corrosion. There are steels that are easier to work or cut, and there are steels that are so hard that they are almost impossible to work under ordinary conditions. Steel can be purchased in a wide variety of shapes and sizes.

To understand where steel comes from and what it is, you have to first look at the element iron. Iron is the major raw material used to make steel. Steel contains about 98% iron, 1.7% carbon (more or less), and a very small percentage of other elements. The exact amount of each element determines the properties desired.

Components of Steel

By far the major constituent of steel is iron—an element with the symbol Fe, atomic number 26, and atomic weight 55.847. Iron does not exist in nature in its free state, but is obtained from ore that is mined from the ground. Iron makes up approximately 4–5% of the Earth's crust, although much of it cannot be obtained economically. Iron-oxide ores are mined to make iron and steel. Those principle ores are hematite, limonite, magnetite, and the low-grade taconite.

Although various elements such as chromium, nickel, manganese, molybdenum, silicon, titanium, and vanadium may or may not be added to the iron to make different types of steel, the only essential one is carbon.

Carbon is everywhere; it is an essential element in all living things. Coal is made of carbon. Diamonds are made of carbon. The so-called lead in lead pencils is not really lead, it is graphite which is a form of carbon. Carbon has the symbol C, the atomic number 6, and an atomic weight of 12.01115.

Buyer confusion about the types and components of steel can occur because steel is often classified as either carbon steel, alloy steel, high speed steel, tool steel, or stainless steel, even though by definition all steel must contain carbon. In fact, even various types of what we call iron are not pure iron, but contain carbon. Pure iron would not contain any other element since it is an element itself. What differentiates iron from steel and the various classifications of steel is the percentage of carbon the metal contains. Technically, alloys are any steel that contains more than trace amounts of elements other than iron and carbon. However, stainless and tool steels may be categorized separately because of the special constituents and the percentages they contain.

Alloy steels, that is, those containing added elements, are produced for special purposes. Steels can be made to resist corrosion by adding copper during the manufacturing process. Others are produced to withstand heat.

Still others are produced to be especially strong by using relatively larger amounts of nickel, chromium, molybdenum, and vanadium. Adding sulfur in the steel-making process makes the finished product easier to machine.

Properties of Steel

If you asked the average person to describe the properties of steel, he or she would probably say it is hard. He or she might add that it has a metallic appearance and that it shines and has a silvery color when not painted. All this is true, but there is so much more. Steel is not just hard. Diamonds are very hard and they are made of carbon, but diamonds are brittle and will break into many pieces when struck by a hammer. They will also burn in a hot fire. Steel, on the other hand, is not brittle. It can be bent without breaking. "The malleability of steel distinguishes it from cast iron and pig iron; initial malleability when cast distinguishes steel from malleable cast iron; hardenability by rapid cooling distinguishes steel from wrought iron."[1] Steel can withstand high temperatures. With the right chemistry, it can withstand corrosive materials and resist rust. It can be made to be elastic and used to make springs.

To fully understand the properties of iron, steel, and other metals, you need to know something about atomic theory. Knowing the molecular structure of steel helps one understand why steel fractures under certain conditions, why it changes states, and why various manufacturing processes change its behavior. Different types of steel are made by adding small quantities of other elements or taking away some other elements that are present as impurities.

Changes in the properties of steel are obtained by heating the raw material to different temperatures, or at other times by reheating, quenching, and cooling the metal. The properties of the metal are changed by pounding or pressing. They are changed or made different by cutting or forming in one direction rather than another. To understand why this is so and why steel behaves differently under stress, it is necessary to know something about the crystal structure of the metal.

In the cooling and solidification process as the metal is produced, atoms form crystals and grow complex lattices that are referred to as dendrites. These lattices vary in size and shape depending on the processes and type of steel. Grains that may not have symmetrical shapes are formed from the crystals. A grain boundary is an area having space lattices arranged differently than nearby grains. Grain size is determined by the rate of cooling of the metal. Rapid cooling results in smaller grain size. Working the metal and reheating change the grain size, shape, and orientation of the grains. These changes, known as plastic deformation, are caused by slip or the shifting of the crystals within a plane. The strength of the metal is a function of grain size, shape, and orientation.[2]

You Need Iron Before You Make Steel

Iron is obtained from ore mined out of the ground. Iron ore has been obtained from the Great Lakes region for close to 100 years, with the amount mined ranging from slightly over 30 million tons to over 90 million tons. In recent years, the amount has been between 50 and 60 million metric tons, except for 1932 when only a little more than 3.5 million tons were mined. In 1993, usable production is estimated at 55.2 million metric tons.[3] Not too long ago, the leading areas of production in the United States were the mines in the Mesabi Range in Minnesota and in Michigan. Today, high production areas are in Indiana, New Jersey, Ohio, and Pennsylvania. There are also mines elsewhere around the United States and in Canada. World production of iron ore is now over 900 million tons. There are over a dozen countries producing ore. The U.S. was the leading producer of iron ore before the 1960s when the Soviet Union became the leader. Other countries now producing more ore than the United States include Australia, Brazil, and China.

How Iron Is Made

To obtain iron, you need to heat the iron-containing ore to a high temperature in order to remove other elements. Iron ore is made up of iron, oxygen, and undesirable elements. There are different types of ore that come from different areas.

Low-grade ore goes through a process referred to as "beneficiating the ore." This improves the quality of the raw material. There are various steps used in the process depending on the type of ore and the type of steel being made. Basically it involves washing, screening, grinding to a powder, and baking.

Some raw material is obtained by "sintering." Certain ores as well as flue dust from a blast-furnace are sintered by mixing them with powdered coal or coke and passing air through them to facilitate combustion. The result is a material that can be used in the blast-furnace with higher grade ore material.

Figure 5-1. Charging hot metal BOP. (Courtesy of National Steel.)

Iron that is referred to as pig iron, because it was cast in ingots called pigs, is produced by a blast-furnace. This type of furnace consists of a large cylindrical receptacle over 100 feet high and 40 feet in diameter, in addition to three or more large chambers used to heat the air used by the furnace to 1800°F. The ore — along with sintered material, coke, and limestone — is loaded into the furnace. The "blast" part of the name comes from the fact that the hot air is forced into the furnace to create a high temperature and enhance combustion. The furnace is lined with firebrick ceramic material to withstand the high continuous heat. To maintain the necessary high temperatures at minimum cost, blast-furnaces seldom shut down except for repairs and routine maintenance, which may take days to complete.

There are other methods of producing iron, such as by using gas instead of coke as the fuel. The result is an iron product free from some of the impurities present in iron produced by the blast-furnace, and which is better suited for making high-grade steels. Another method of making almost pure iron is by using electrolysis.

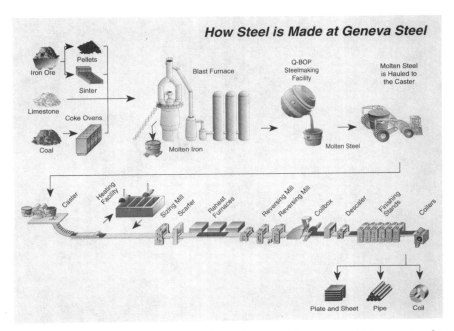

Figure 5-2. Process of iron and steel production. (Courtesy of Geneva Steel.)

How Steel Is Made

Steel can be made by using all newly produced iron, by using some newly produced iron and some scrap metal, or by using all scrap metal. It is most common to use scrap in the production of steel. Therefore, the availability and price of scrap is a determining factor in the cost and price of new steel.

Before the Bessemer process (invented in the late 1850s), steel was made in small quantities by placing iron bars in a crucible and melting them with charcoal, or placing the bars in a charcoal furnace. At that time, production was measured in pounds rather than tons.

Until fairly recently, the Siemens–Martin open-hearth process, which was invented in about 1860, was used to make most of the steel in the United States. Mills have now converted to the more efficient basic oxygen process (BOP, see Figure 5-1) or use electric arc furnaces. In the basic oxygen process, molten iron and scrap are placed in the vessel. Then an oxygen lance is inserted and pure oxygen is blown at high speeds into the furnace. Impurities are reduced and the molten iron is converted to steel as the oxy-

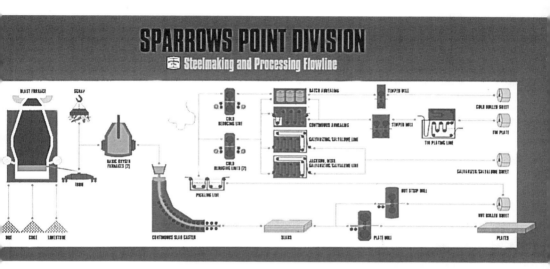

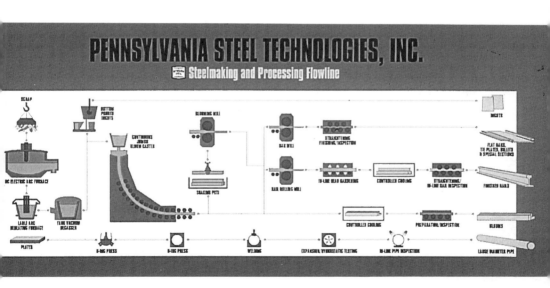

Figure 5-2, continued. (Courtesy of Geneva Steel.)

gen combines with carbon. The steel from the basic oxygen furnace moves to the ladle metallurgy facility (LMF) for further refining by changing the chemistry and using electrodes to increase the temperature. The molten steel from the LMF is then sent to continuous slab casters. Formerly, ingots were made and then sent to the primary rolling mills. Continuous casting eliminates this step and thereby reduces cost. The slab from the continuous caster is sent to the hot strip mills and processed into coils and sheets of various types (see the flowchart of steel-making processes).

Steel Prices and Scrap Used in Steel Making

The availability of iron and steel scrap and prices of scrap metal affect the price of new steel. Scrap metal is important because it is used in the production of new metal. The mini-mills rely heavily on scrap to produce new steel; therefore,the effect of scrap prices on mini-mill producers is greater than it is for the larger integrated mills. As scrap prices increase, the integrated mills become more and more competitive.

In 1993, the reported estimated consumption of iron and steel scrap was 68 million metric tons at an average price of $106.09 per metric ton delivered.[4]

Production and Use of Slag

Slag is a byproduct of iron and steel-making. Steel slags from open-hearth, basic oxygen, and electric arc furnaces were processed at 70 facilities in 25 states. The amount of iron slag produced is declining because of blast-furnace closings. Some of the material is recycled to blast-furnaces, directly or as agglomerates, as a source of iron and flux materials. Iron slag was typically used as road base. The estimated production of slag in the United States in 1993 was approximately 22 million tons valued at $136 million.[5]

Using Steel and Changing Its Properties

When steel is worked by forging, casting, or cutting, it changes its properties. It may become so hard that it is impossible to work anymore or loses some of the desired characteristics of that type of steel. Likewise, the steel as purchased may not have the properties desired: it may be too hard or too soft. The desired hardness or softness is obtained by what is called "heat treating." The process of heating the steel or cooling it changes the distribution of the carbon atoms. The process involves raising the steel to the proper temperature, keeping it at that temperature for the correct length of time, and then cooling the steel at a controlled rate. Each type of steel and the desired properties require a different temperature and a different length of time. Companies specialize in providing heat-treating services. Some have highly trained metallurgists, engineers, or other highly experienced and well-qualified personnel to do the work properly and guarantee results. Other heat-treating companies have limited capabilities and should only be used for work well within their knowledge and experience. The buyer should investigate the source's background and capabilities, and should ask for references and check the references carefully before sending work to a new source.

Once in a while, a piece of metal used in production or service fails; and disputes arise between the buyer, the manufacturer of the metal, and the heat-treating company. These can be avoided by requiring testing and documentation of testing at each phase in the production and use of the metal. An additional help in preventing problems or speeding their resolution is to eliminate as many unneeded people or extra suppliers as possible. The purchasing manager can help by assigning metal purchases and subcontracting work such as heat-treating services to one person if the volume of transactions permits. Where it is possible to obtain a finished product from one source, it is best to have the manufacturer control their own heat-treating needs, even if it means they will subcontract the work. In that way, they are fully responsible for the end product and can blame no one else for failures.

Terms Used in the Metal-Working Industry

The buyer of metals should be familiar with the following terms used in the metal-working and heat-treating industries.

Air Hardening: To harden a steel by cooling in air, or a type of steel so hardened.

Annealing or Tempering: Heating and cooling a material to remove internal stresses.

Carburizing: To harden the surface of steel by heating it in contact with a carbon material.

Cyaniding: To harden a ferrous alloy by coming in contact with molten cyanide. Cyanide has the chemical symbol CN; in other words, it contains carbon and nitrogen.

Flame Hardening: A process of hardening the surface of steel by using a flame at a controlled rate.

Induction Hardening: A method of hardening a metal by heating it through electromagnetic induction and then quenching.

Nitriding: Hardening the surface of steel by heating and introducing nitrogen that combines to form nitrides.

Normalizing: A heat-treating process which relieves stresses caused by cold working or by welding. The steel is cooled in air and cooled more rapidly than in full tempering to obtain a harder steel that has greater tensile strength.

Oil Hardening: Hardening steel after heating and cooling slowly in oil.

Surface Hardening: As the name implies, it is a process of making the surface of steel harder by various processes such as carburizing, nitriding, or flame hardening.

Stress Relieving: A process of heating steel to a low temperature and then cooling to relieve stresses caused by various metal-working operations. The process helps prevent warpage and cracking when the material is heat treated.

The Steel-Making Industry in the United States

Like so many mature industries, steel companies have been struggling to survive for a long time. This author remembers steel salespeople complaining decades ago about their companies not making any money and the low prices that needed to be increased. At the same time, they were paying both their salaried and hourly workers top dollar. According to them, the unions were negotiating work rules that restricted management's ability to run the companies efficiently.

After World War II, international companies began to produce steel from newer plants and to export to this country. The domestic steel industry began to lose significant amounts of business because of the lower prices that could be obtained from imported steel. For example, this author obtained tool steel from Europe at 46% less than could be purchased domestically.

Domestic producers accused some foreign sources of "dumping," that is, of exporting at prices below their domestic price. In addition, the domestic producers pointed out that foreign governments were subsidizing their producers. Eventually, our government put pressure on the foreign producers to curtail their exports. Today, the amount of foreign steel has tapered off, but some of the domestic mills and service centers are owned by foreign steel companies. Others have joint ventures with domestic producers.

Steel companies are now more efficient. They have negotiated more realistic labor contracts. They have introduced modern methods and equipment to cut costs. Although the United States has given up first place in production of steel, the industry is in a better position to compete.

Nevertheless, some of the producers are still losing money. Many of the companies are still not customer or marketing oriented. Years ago, steel salespeople called on every potential or actual customer in order to get any small amount of business. When some smart financial type figured out that the cost of those sales calls exceeded any possible profit, such selling methods were eliminated. The mills no longer were interested in the small customer. Service centers were the place you had to go to obtain what you needed.

But the pendulum swung too far. When I was the largest independent purchaser of tin plate in the United States, I recall trying to obtain prices from one of the top mills in the nation, without any success. Even after a call to one of their top executives, and after receiving profuse apologies for not responding, they still neglected to submit a bid.

It is certainly not unique to the steel business, but less-than-aggressive marketing and sales practices still exist. Evidence of that is the list of primary steel suppliers at the end of the next chapter. These are the ones that responded with information. Out of 25 companies, only 10 bothered to answer. This was in spite of several letters and even telephone calls.

Nevertheless, the future of the steel industry looks bright, costs are continuing to be reduced, and the trend to substitute other products for steel seems to be reversed. For example, "According to Ford Motor Company the average vehicle built in 1993 contained 1,726 pounds of steel, up from 1,710 pounds in 1992, marking the second consecutive yearly increase... The residential construction sector is potentially a rich market for steel producers. Steel framing for houses is being promoted as a light-weight alternative to wood framing. A galvanized steel frame for a 2000 square foot house would weigh approximately one-fourth the weight of a lumber structure."[6]

Footnotes

[1] *Elementary Metallurgy and Metallography*, by Arthur M. Shrager, published by Dover Publications, Inc., New York, 1969, p. 75

[2] For a full discussion of this important subject and an excellent background for metal and metal product purchasing, see *Elementary Metallurgy and Metallography*, referred to in footnote 1.

[3] Mineral Commodity Summaries, 1994, United States Department of the Interior, Bureau of Mines, Prepared by Cheryl C. Solomon (202) 501-9393, FAX (202) 501-3751, pp. 88–89.

[4] Mineral Commodity Summaries, 1994, United States Department of the Interior, Bureau of Mines, Prepared by Cheryl C. Solomon (202) 501-9393, FAX (202) 501-3751, pp. 92–93.

[5] Mineral Commodity Summaries, 1994, United States Department of the Interior, Bureau of Mines, Prepared by Cheryl C. Solomon (202) 501-9393, FAX (202) 501-3751, p. 94.

[6] U.S. Industrial Outlook, 1994, U.S. Department of Commerce, International Trade Administration.

CHAPTER 6

Types of Steel Products, Source Selection, Ordering, and Obtaining Proper Quality

Where the Buyer Can Obtain Steel

Steel can be obtained from various sources. The two most usual types of suppliers are service centers and (directly from) mills producing the steel. Service centers are a type of "middlemen." The *Thomas Register of American Manufacturers*[1] lists over 400 service centers spread out in cities across the United States. They range in size from one million dollars in assets to over one-hundred million dollars in assets. Some are divisions of steel manufacturers, others are independent. These service centers are sometimes referred to as distributors or warehouses. Buyers usually differentiate between the two principal sources by referring to the products as mill steel or warehouse steel. More recently, the use of the term "service center" has replaced the term "warehouse." This is probably because such suppliers do more than simply store the material. They often cut sizes for specific customers and divide large quantities into small quantities for the customer who only uses a small amount of any one type and/or only orders infrequently.

Some service centers, such as Central Steel and Ryerson, carry huge inventories of a large variety of metal products. Some carry various other metals besides steel. Other warehouses specialize in a few types of material.

There are only a relatively few mills in the United States. Steel mill sources can be divided into the fully integrated mill that processes ore into iron and then many types of steel, and mini-mills that use scrap to make new steel. There are hundreds of service centers throughout the United States. In addition, there are steel producers in a number of foreign countries.

Other categories of sellers are the manufacturer's representatives and brokers. These are small firms which, most of the time, act as middlemen to get what you need from the sources they represent or from various sources who are happy to receive your order. In the majority of cases, representatives and brokers keep no inventory and have no plant facilities. All they have is a desk and a telephone.

Although brokers may have in-depth experience in the steel industry, they usually (but not always) sell secondary material of inferior quality. If you are willing to take the risk, and if your quality demands are not high, you sometimes can obtain material at a substantial discount through these sources.

If your requirements are relatively small and you are located in a remote area, a skilled manufacturer's representative can be a great help in responding to your needs. He or she may represent several different types of mills specializing in different types of products. A representative provides a valuable service to mini-mills and others who cannot justify full time salaries for salespeople calling on small usage customers or those located in remote areas with little chance of obtaining much business.

How You Decide Which Type of Source to Use

Before you can decide on which type of source to use, you must know or estimate your expected usage and the type of steel you want to buy. You also must consider the amount of storage space you have or are willing to use to store the material. As is true in almost any type of buying, if you can cut out middlemen, you are better off. But that is somewhat of an oversimplification, because there are a number of factors to consider before you assume that buying from the mill is the best choice.

First of all, you must have the need for a fairly large quantity before the mill will even consider selling to you. If you are only buying a few pieces of steel or if you measure your requirements in pounds, you will need to go to a service center to get your requirements.

Second, you must take delivery of a large quantity all at one time — not necessarily the entire order, but a significant amount. You will need special handling equipment to move heavy bundles or coils. Some mills will produce smaller coils so your equipment will be able to handle it, but even the smallest coil requires mechanical devices.

Finally, in most cases, when you order from the mill, you need to be able to live with a long lead time. Mills don't keep much (if any) inventory; therefore, you must wait until the type of steel you want is scheduled to be produced. This might be twelve to sixteen weeks in the future or longer. Lead times can become even longer if you want to buy from an international source, because you have to add transit time for overseas shipments, as well as time to clear customs. Foreign mills, to some extent, have overcome this obstacle by establishing their own service centers that warehouse inventory from their mills. However, foreign-owned service centers don't always stock material from foreign mills, or stock every steel product that you may need. Some foreign-owned service centers primarily stock material from domestic mills and are therefore sources for domestic material only.

In addition to the above constraints, there may be advantages to ordering from a service center. Many service centers will perform secondary operations that most mills are not willing or equipped to do. If you need either a large quantity or a small quantity of a certain shape cut out of plate, many service centers will be happy to do the job for you. Of course, there is a charge for extra operations. Some, if not most, service centers will also stock special material used by only a single customer.

Specifying and Ordering Steel

There are so many types of steel, and so much data required to precisely describe a particular type of steel, that a buyer may be daunted by the task. In addition, there is more than one organization that has established standards used by engineers and industry. The job of writing a complete and adequate description is further complicated because suppliers request still different information, or supply different nomenclature to data, or give proprietary names to their own grade of steel. For example, some steel producers produce their own chemistry for a steel designed for a certain purpose. In other words, they establish their own formula with unique percentages of the various elements going into a particular type of steel. For all practical purposes, the steel may be so close to another standard product widely available in the marketplace that the user will not be able to tell the difference. But once that proprietary name has been placed on drawings or is used by the buying company's engineers, it is often difficult to convince users that the steel is not significantly different from a less expensive alternative.

Suppliers sometimes color code different types of steel, so the user can easily distinguish one type of steel from another. The problem with this is that there is no standard color code. One supplier may use one color for a type of steel and another supplier may use another. For example, Wisconsin Steel and Tube Corporation codes 1045 steel blue, whereas Jorgensen Steel & Aluminum uses red for the 1045 and uses blue for HR mild steel bars, for A36 sheets, and for 440C stainless steel bars.

Steel Products

There are so many steel products that it is impossible to list them all in a book of this size and scope; however, here are some broad, general categories that include hundreds of varieties.

Bar: Steel is available in a wide variety of bar sizes and grades from service centers. The bars may be square, rectangular, or octagonal shaped. The service center will cut the bars to the length you want.

Plate: Steel plate is usually a rectangular shape of steel of 3/16" or more in thickness. Plate is usually what is called a mild or low carbon steel. Service centers will shear, flame cut, or laser cut the shape you need. This makes it possible in some cases to use plate in place of more expensive castings and forgings. A careful analysis is required to consider the properties required of the metal and compare the cost of both the tooling and labor. Specifically that includes the cost of patterns, dies, and secondary operations. Plate may be used for many applications such as weldment bases for machine tools, in buildings for construction purposes, and to make various heavy equipment.

Sheet, Strip, and Coil: Sheet and strip differ from plate because they are thinner, they come in many thicknesses, but all less than 3/16" in thickness. Sheet may come in a rectangular shape usually measuring more than 12" in width or in one continuous coil. Coils come in standard

Figure 6-1. Inspection of electrogalvanized steel. (Courtesy of National Steel.)

widths and can be slit by service centers to the width you need. The Coilplus service center in Illinois recently installed laser measuring devices that control the size and consistency with great accuracy. Standard coil weights are considered to be approximately 200 pounds per inch of width; that is, a standard weight coil 2-1/2" X 200# = 500#, where # is used to denote pounds. Sheet, strip, and coil steel are mostly used to make stampings or products that are punched out of the steel and then given various shapes.

To obtain coils to fit a particular need at the lowest cost, it is best to provide the following type of information to the supplier.

Coil Steel Specifications

Grade — Grade information can be presented in different ways. It includes a general description of the type of steel such as cold rolled, hot rolled, pickled, oiled, hot dipped galvanized, electrogalvanized, long terne, tin plate, prepainted, and aluminized. You can use an AISI number, an SAE number, or an analysis number.

Size — Thickness and width information is essential.

Tolerances — Indicate how much your ideal measurement requirements may vary by showing the plus amount and the minus amount. Keep in mind that no product will be exact to any measurement. There is always some variation. If you can accept standard tolerances, you will pay less.

Quantity — Most steel is priced by the pound although it is also purchased by the number of feet. It should be purchased the same way as it is priced. In other words, the quantity should be in the same units of measure as the price. It makes it easier to check and match invoices to the purchase order.

Finish — **Hot rolled, pickled, and oiled** (HRP&O) is the finish for application where a cold rolled finish is not important.

Alternatively, if you need **cold rolled** (C.R.) steel, **dull or satin** is the most common commercial finish. **Commercial bright finish** may be used for certain plating operations, but is not suitable for all plating.

A **luster finish** is the best if bright plating and for items that will be polished or buffed.

Temper — This is the hardness you want.

Packing and Restrictions — Specify if you want the coils wrapped to protect them from the elements during transportation or storage. Indicate maximum size or weight of the coil for material handling.

Coil Specifications — Indicate restrictions on inside and outside diameter of the coil if necessary.

Delivery Date — The date you need the material should be clearly indicated. However, make sure the supplier agrees to the date before you place the order. A supplier's delivery performance should not be measured from a date that is not agreed to by the supplier. Some buyers show two delivery dates — the date agreed to by the seller, and a preferred date if earlier delivery is possible.

Where and How to Ship — Always include the destination of the material. This is especially important if the purchasing office is in a different location than the plant or storage area for the material. Indicate the name of the truck line or mode of transportation if there is a preference. This may be a negotiable item as steel companies usually have their own trucks or contracts with carriers.

Price — The price should be printed on the purchase order and clearly established in the contract. The buyer should do everything possible to obtain a firm price or at least a price that will only fluctuate by a predetermined formula. The prices should be associated with a particular unit of measure such as pounds, tons, base boxes, etc.

F.O.B. Terms — The F.O.B term (Free On Board) indicates where title to the goods passes from buyer to seller. This helps determine who pays for freight and who would file claims against a carrier if there is carrier damage. It is important to realize, however, that wherever title passes the buyer becomes the owner, and not until then. Whoever owns the goods is responsible for the goods, even if those goods are at some distant location. If you purchase goods F.O.B. Gary, IN, and you are located in Atlanta, GA, you become owner when the goods are delivered in Gary, IN, even though you are still in Atlanta, GA. If something happens to those goods along the way, you still must pay the supplier, even though you never received the goods in Atlanta. Naturally sellers want to ship F.O.B. their plants, but buyers should try to negotiate F.O.B. delivered, regardless of who pays for freight.

Other Terms and Conditions — Other terms may include a warranty provision and a requirement for certification of material.

Structurals

Structural shapes may be produced directly by a finishing mill, or may be produced by specialty suppliers that make the desired shapes out of other shapes.

Stainless

Stainless steel is usually produced by mills that specialize in these more expensive types of steel, such as Allegheny Ludlum. Typical specification numbers are 201, 202, 301, etc. Type 201 has 0.15% carbon, from 5.5%–7.5% Mn, a maximum of 1% silicon (Si), a maximum of 0.06% phosphorus (P), a maximum of 0.03% sulfur (S), from 16%-18% chromium (Cr), and 3.5%-5.5% nickel (Ni). Because stainless is more expensive, the volume produced is less. Stainless steels come in various grades—some with a very high resistance to corrosion, others with less resistance. The higher the resistance or quality, the higher the price. But you may not need the highest quality for your application. Unless the product will be exposed to very corrosive chemicals and extreme temperatures, the less expensive grades will do the job. Stainless steel is used for tableware (forks and knives), cutlery, cookware, instruments, appliances, and various other products

Alloys

There are those alloys referred to as High Strength, Low Alloy Steels (HSLA) that differentiate them from tool steels that are also alloys. Alloys are really any products that contain more than one metal and are made for a special purpose. Although low carbon steel may have traces of other elements, the amount is so small that it does not affect the properties. The percentage of nonferrous metals added to carbon steel may not be great, but it is great enough to change the properties. Because some of the alloying elements are expensive and because the manufacturing processes may be more difficult, alloys are more expensive than carbon steel.

High-Speed and Tool Steel

Although tool steels are alloys, they are often classified separately because of their special uses. Tool steels such as H12 are used to make die casting dies and aluminum extrusion dies; H13 is used to make die casting dies and stamping dies and forging tools. High-speed steels such as M1 and M2 are used to make twist drills and milling cutters. T4 is used to make gear cutters and shavers, milling cutters, hobs, and toolbits. The letter symbols in the AISI designation of steels refer to various types.

Types of Steel and Letter Designation	Alloying Element or Type
Cold Work Tool Steels	
A	Medium alloy air hardening
D	High carbon, high chromium
O	Oil hardening
Hot Work Tool Steels	
H1-H19	Chromium
H20-H39	Tungsten
H40-H59	Molybdenum

Shock resisting tool steels carry the prefix S; mold steels carry the prefix P; special purpose tool steels carry the prefix L for low alloy types, and F for carbon tungsten types; and water hardening tool steels carry the prefix W.

Tin Mill Products

By far the largest percentage of tin usage (tin is an element) is in the production of tin plate, which is really low carbon steel with a very thin coat of tin to prevent rust. This is the reason that tin mill products are included with other steel products. Furthermore, tin plate is produced by some of the major steel mills. Also, so-called "other tin mill products" don't contain any tin, but they are called tin mill products because they are made in the same facilities as the tin plate. The principal noncoated tin product is called black plate and is simply flat rolled steel.

Tin plate is produced electrolytically by feeding coils of flat rolled steel into a bath containing bars of tin. An electric current is passed through the bath using one of the bars as the cathode, and the tin migrates to the sheet of steel as it passes through.

Most tin is mined outside of the United States. Major sources for imported tin have been Brazil, Bolivia, China, and Indonesia. The U.S. Bureau of Mines says that the major use of tin is for cans and containers, which amounts to 32%; followed by 22% for electrical; 10% for construction; 11% for transportation; and 25% for other purposes such as solder, to make bronze, to make other alloys, and miscellaneous applications.

1993 World Mine Production and Reserves of Tin[2]

Location	Mine Production	Reserves
United States	Negligible	—
Australia	6,000	210,000
Bolivia	15,000	450,000
Brazil	30,000	1,200,000
China	43,000	1,600,000
Indonesia	25,000	750,000
Malaysia	14,000	1,200,000
Peru	6,000	20,000
Portugal	7,000	70,000
Russia	10,000	300,000
Thailand	14,000	940,000
Zaire	2,000	510,000
Other countries	2,000	180,000
World Total (rounded)	175,000[3]	7,000,000

Tin Pricing

Naturally, if you buy tin, you want to keep tabs on the price of tin in the marketplace; but buyers of tin plate do not need to know the price of tin since tin is only a thin layer of material on the steel. Nevertheless, the cost of tin is one of the components of the total price and, therefore, it is a good idea to be aware of the price movement of tin if you buy any appreciable amount of tin plate. Be assured, if the price of tin rises dramatically, you can expect to see a rise in the price of tin plate. Conversely, if you see the price of tin fall precipitously, you have a good case for some price reduction of tin plate.

Between 1989 and the spring of 1995, the average price of tin ranged from a low of $2.32 per pound in London to a high New York composite price of $5.20 per pound. The composite price on May 3, 1995 was $4.01 as reported by the *Wall Street Journal* and taken from *Metals Week*.

Steel Pricing

Most steel is purchased by weight — usually the "pound" is the unit of measure. There is a base price for the grade or type of steel you want. Prices vary widely depending on type, grade, the amount you buy, and various extras that apply to different processes, specifications, or quality levels. Extra charges may apply because of size, tolerances, finish, temper, and packing requirements. Low carbon steel is the least expensive. Alloys, stainless, high-speed steels, and tool steels are more expensive. Exotic alloys can be very expensive. The base price of steel changes infrequently, and suppliers in the industry normally increase or decrease prices at the same time. Published or announced prices may not actually be charged, and price increase announcements have often been rescinded. Salespeople will tell buyers that there is going to be an increase in a certain month. The alleged purpose of this is to permit the buyer to order before the increase goes into effect. Sometimes those predicted increases happen, sometimes they don't.

Buyers who use a lot of steel are wise to periodically obtain prices from more than one source. Prices can also be obtained by subscribing to a service from the *American Metal Market*.

Prices of all steel products do not necessarily go up at once. Low carbon steel may increase, whereas tool steel will remain constant, or vice versa. Prices from the mill may go up, but the price from a service center may not change at once. It all depends on what you can negotiate. When you buy, make sure you get the price broken down by each charge so both the price and the need for that feature can be properly evaluated.

Pricing Tin Plate

Although the price of steel is normally by weight, that is not true of tin plate. Even though a requestor may ask for so many pounds of tin plate, the supplier sells it by what is called a "base box" and that is the way the buyer should place the order. A base box equals an area amounting to 31,360 square inches or 217.78 square feet. In Europe, a metric unit of measure called a "SITA" (System International Tinplate Area) is used, and it amounts to 100 square meters.

Getting the Quality You Want

The first time to discuss quality issues is before you use any supplier. This is as true with the purchase of steel as it is with any other product. Specifying a higher type of steel does not mean that the delivered product will measure up to what you are paying for. In fact, the management of one company I worked for insisted that I get a higher level of quality than published for a particular grade. It was tough to get the suppliers to agree, but they did provide us with much better quality than we had a right to expect for the price we were paying.

If steel is used in a part or assembly that fails because of poor quality, the company that sells that item can be subjected to expensive lawsuits and huge settlements. One way that the buyer can partially protect his or her company is to ask for certification from the steel producer. Surprisingly, only about 5–10 percent of buyers request such documentation. One reason could be that they only see such documentation as evidence of getting a good quality product, forgetting the possible legal protection offered by certification. On the other hand, reliance on such certification for good quality may not be enough. Mills only take samples for testing from the head of the heat.

Steel Shipments by Product Type	% [4]
Distributors or Service Centers	25.43
Construction	14.58
Automotive	13.22
Processing	11.00
Exports	5.11
Containers	4.74
Electrical Equipment	2.55
Machinery	2.33
Appliances	1.79
Oil & Gas	1.73
Other Equipment	1.00
Other	16.52
Total	100.00

Steel Manufacturing Sources and Company Profiles

Allegheny Ludlum Corporation
1000 Six PPG Place
Pittsburgh, PA 15222-5479
(412) 394-2800 FAX (412) 394-3034

Eastern Regional Sales Office
P.O. Box 1409, 80 Valley Street
Wallingford, CT 06492
(203) 265-9166

Western Regional Sales Office
1501 Woodfield Drive, Suite 408 South
Schaumburg, IL 60173
(708) 605-9190

Jessop Specialty Products
500 Green Street
Washington, PA 15301
(412) 222-4000

Allegheny Ludlum is a major producer of an extensive range of flat rolled specialty materials—stainless steels, silicon electrical steels, tool steels, and other advanced alloys. These highly engineered materials are produced in more than 150,000 combinations of different properties, chemistries, processing routes, finishes, forms, sizes, and other special characteristics.

Sales in 1994 were $1076.9 million. Of that, 78% was for stainless products, 13% silicon electrical steel, and 9% other specialty alloys. Net income was $18.2 million. The company has approximately 6000 employees in its plants and offices in 18 locations and 8 states; this includes the Washington, PA, plant, formerly Jessop Steel, which was acquired in November 1994.

Bethlehem Steel Corporation

1170 Eighth Avenue
Bethlehem, PA 18016-7699
(215) 694-2424 FAX (215) 694-5743

Two divisions, Burns Harbor, located in Indiana on Lake Michigan about 50 miles southeast of Chicago, IL, and Sparrows Point, located on the Chesapeake Bay near Baltimore, MD, account for over 80% of the steel sold by Bethlehem Steel. These divisions produce flat rolled steel products. Shipments of sheets, including high value added products such as coated sheets and tin plate, accounted for 68% of the steel segment; and Bethlehem is the country's largest producer of steel plate, which accounted for 14% of the steel segment sales in 1994.

Another division is Bethlehem Structural Products Corporation which produces structural steel shapes and piling primarily for the construction market. This is the only domestic producer of hot rolled sheet piling used in retaining walls and piers.

Pennsylvania Steel Technologies, Inc. is another unit of Bethlehem. It uses electric furnace steel-making and a continuous caster for the production of railroad rails for the rail transportation industry, specialty blooms for the forging industry, and flat bars. It is one of only two rail producers in the United States. PST also produces large-diameter pipe for the oil and gas industries.

Bethlehem also has various other plants and facilities. Annual sales revenue for 1994 was $4819.4 million, and net income before income taxes and cumulative effect of changes in accounting was $94.5 million or $80.5 after provision for income taxes. The average number of employees in 1994 was 19,900.

Geneva Steel
P.O. Box 2500
Provo, UT 84603
(801) 227-9174 FAX (801) 227-9431

Geneva Steel is the only integrated steel mill operating west of the Mississippi River. Located 45 miles south of Salt Lake City, the company manufactures hot rolled steel plate, sheet, and pipe for sale primarily in the western and central United States. The company acquired the steel mill and related facilities in a leveraged buyout from USX Corporation in August 1987. The company's principal properties consist of the approximately 1400-acre site on which the steel mill and related facilities are located, the company's iron ore mines in southern Utah, and the limestone quarry near the steel mill.

Net sales for fiscal 1994 were $486,062,000 with a net loss of $26,230. The company's modernization efforts are designed to increase throughput, reduce costs, and improve quality. The following major capital projects have been recently completed or are presently underway: the continuous casting facility, which converts liquid steel into slabs; the wide coiled plate project, which includes facilities for the production of wide coiled plate and for the further processing and handling of plate products; the rolling mill finishing stand improvements, which will improve the shape and gauge of finished products and increase rolling mill throughput; additional slab heating facilities, which will increase slab temperature immediately prior to rolling; and a plasma-fired cupola iron-making facility.

Laclede Steel Company
One Metropolitan Square
St. Louis, MO 63102
(314) 425-1400

Sales Offices
(800) 325-2663
In Missouri (800) 392-7769 FAX (314) 425-1534

Laclede Steel manufactures high-quality carbon and alloy steel in two 225-ton electric furnaces. Products include cold drawn wire, continuous weld pipe, electric resistance welded tubing, hot rolled products, and welded chain. The hot rolled products include alloy and special quality bars, flat bars, narrow plate, strip, coiled rods, forging billets, and coiled rebars. The mill is in Alton, IL, but shipments are available from plants or depots located in Atlanta, GA; Baltimore, MD; Dallas, TX; Benwood, WV; Alton, IL; Memphis, TN; Fremont, IN; Maryville, MO; and Portland, OR. The sales office is centralized in St. Louis. The company's annual capacity is 900,000 tons.

The LTV Corporation
25 West Prospect Avenue
Cleveland, OH 44115
(216) 622-5000

Sales Offices
Flat Rolled Products
Chicago, IL (708) 364-0710
Cincinnati, OH (513) 745-2300
Cleveland, OH (216) 292-4900
Detroit, MI (810) 736-7500
Kansas City, KS (913) 661-0034
Nashville, TN (615) 371-6700

Sales Office
Tin Mill Products
1-800-462-4684

Sales Office
Tubular Products
1-800-445-7473

LTV is a fully integrated steel producer that ranks as the third largest steel operation in the United States, and the second largest domestic producer of flat rolled steel. The company currently supplies about 20% of the flat rolled steel purchased by the U.S. automotive, appliance, and electrical equipment industries.

Principal products include hot rolled, cold rolled, and coated steel sheet, as well as tubular and tin mill products. LTV is a 100% continuous cast producer, the largest supplier of carbon electrical steels, the largest producer of electrolytically galvanized steel sheets, the largest producer of new ultra-low carbon steels, the largest producer of welded steel pipe and tubing products, and the third largest producer of tin mill products.

LTV operates two integrated steel mills (Cleveland Works and Indiana Harbor Works) and various finishing and processing facilities. Sales of steel mill products accounted for approximately 93% of LTV's 1994 sales.

In December 1994, LTV announced the signing of a letter of intent with Sumitomo Metal Industries, Ltd. and British Steel plc to create a joint venture company. The joint venture will construct and operate a technologically advanced flat rolled mini-mill known as Trico Steel in the southeastern United States with the capacity to produce 2.2 million tons annually of high quality hot rolled steel. Trico Steel will be 50% owned by LTV, with Sumitomo and British Steel each holding 25% interests.

Net sales revenue in 1994 for LTV was $4529.2 million, net income after taxes was $127.1 million. The company has approximately 16,500 employees, of which 15,300 are in steel operations.

Lukens Inc.
50 South First Avenue
Coatesville, PA 19320-0911
(215) 383-3295 FAX (215) 383-2436

Lukens, a 185-year-old fully integrated steel producer, consists of two groups—the Lukens Steel Group which produces carbon, alloy and clad plate in a broad range of grades and sizes; and the recently acquired Washington Stainless Group. The company has steel-making facilities in Coatesville, PA, and Houston, TX; rolling mill operations in three locations, and finishing operations in four locations. It is the third largest producer of plate in North America. Washington Steel produces stainless steel sheet, strip, and plate. Washington Specialty Metals processes and distributes stainless sheet and strip from seven locations in the United States and Canada.

Combined net sales in 1994 were $947 million, and the company's average number of employees was 4060.

National Steel Corporation

4100 Edison Lakes Parkway
Mishawaka, IN 46545-3440
(219) 273-7000

National Steel is the fourth largest integrated steel company in the United States, with shipment of more than 5 million tons of flat rolled products. The company has production facilities in Ecorse, MI, near Detroit, and Portage, IN, in addition to the main facility in Granite City, in the Illinois/Missouri/St. Louis Metropolitan Area. It employs about 9300 people.

The Granite City Division is a leading supplier of high-quality, low-cost flat rolled carbon sheet steel products used for tubing, pipe, automotive, appliance, and construction applications. The division also produces galvanized steel roofing and siding under the names of Strongbarn, Strongbarn II, Strongpanel, and Strongtrim.

In 1994, sales of $2.7 billion represent an increase of 12 percent from $2.4 billion in 1993. Net income for 1994 totaled $168.5 million, compared to a net loss of $258.9 million in 1993. Raw steel production totaled a record 5,763,000 net tons in 1994, up 4 percent from the 5,551,000 net tons produced in the previous year.

Nucor Corporation

2100 Rexford Road
Charlotte, NC 28211
(704) 366-7000
(704) 362-4208

Nucor Steel Division of Nucor Corporation
P.O. Box 311
Crawfordsville, IN 47033
(317) 364-1323
(800) 777-0950
FAX (317) 364-5302

As reported on form 10K to the Securities and Exchange Commission, principal operating facilities and products produced at each location are as follows.

Blytheville-Hickman, AR	2,600,000	Steel shapes, flat rolled
Norfolk-Stanton, NE	1,930,000	Steel shapes, joists & deck
Brigham City-Plymouth, UT	1,700,000	Steel shapes, joists & grinding balls
Darlington-Florence, SC	1,540,000	Steel shapes, joists & deck
Grapeland-Jewett, TX	1,340,000	Steel shapes, joists & deck
Crawfordsville, IN	1,100,000	Flat rolled steel

Additional operating facilities are located in Fort Payne, AL; Saint Joe and Waterloo, IN; and Wilson, NC; all facilities are engaged in the manufacture of steel products. There about 5900 employees in the steel products business. Annual sales for 1993 were $2,253,738,311 and net earnings after taxes were $123,509,607.

Oregon Steel Mills, Inc.
1000 Broadway Building, Suite 2200
1000 S.W. Broadway
Portland, OR 97205
(503) 240-5776

Oregon Steel, formerly Gilmore Steel Corporation, changed to its present name in 1987. The company has five plant locations, which include two steel mills. During 1993 the company established the Portland and CF&I steel mills, and the related downstream finishing facilities, as separate business units to be known as the Oregon Steel Division and the CF&I Steel Division.

The Oregon Steel Division is centered on the company's Portland, OR steel mini-mill (the "Portland Steel Mill"), which supplies steel for the company's steel plate and large diameter pipe finishing facilities. The Portland Steel Mill operates under the name of Oregon Steel Mills, Inc.

The Portland Steel Mill is the only hot rolled steel plate mini-mill and one of two steel plate producers located in the eleven western states.

The company produces eight steel products which include most standard grades of steel plate, a wide range of higher margin specialty steel plate, large-diameter steel pipe, ERW pipe, long length and standard rails, OCTG, wire rod, wire, and bar products. Production capacities at the company's facilities are affected by product mix; however, at the end of 1993, the company had the following nominal capacities.

Location		Capacity(tons)	Production (tons)
Portland Steel Mill	Melting	800,000	800,000
	Rolling	450,000	372,200
Fontana Plate Mill	Rolling	750,000	331,600
Napa Facility	Steel Pipe	350,000	133,700
Camrose Facility	Steel Pipe	326,000	154,000
Pueblo Steel Mill	Melting	1,000,000	913,500
	Finishing Mill	1,500,000	828,800

Sales for 1994 were $838,268,000 and new income after taxes was $12,068,000. There were 3060 full time employees.

Weirton Steel Corporation
400 Three Springs Drive
Weirton, WV 26062-4989
(304) 797-2000
Sales (800) 223-9777

All operating facilities are at the Weirton location with a raw steel production capacity of approximately 3 million tons. Products include flat rolled carbon steels in sheet and strip form. These products are sold chiefly as hot rolled, cold rolled or coated products, including hot dipped and electro-galvanized steels and tin mill products. Annual sales for 1993 were $1,201,093,000 and the net loss was $229,242,000. The number of employees was 6026.

Steel Service Centers

Coilplus-Illinois, Inc.
2001 Coilplus Drive
P.O. Box 280
Plainfield, IL 60544
(815) 436-3999 FAX (815) 436-3299 TELEX 248054 COIL IL UR

Coilplus-Alabama
P.O. Box 567
107 Durham Drive

Athens, AL 35611
(205) 233-3550

Coilplus-Ohio
4801 Gateway Boulevard
Springfield, OH 45502
(513) 322-4455

Precision Coil Processing
Milnor 4 Bleigh
P.O. Box 11158
Philadelphia, PA 19136
(215) 331-5200

Jorgensen Steel & Aluminum
Baltimore (301) 850-4444
Boston (508) 435-6854
Buffalo (716) 876-4700
Charlotte (704) 596-6116
Chicago (708) 307-6100
Cincinnati (513) 771-3223
Cleveland (216) 291-5555
Dallas (214) 741-1761
Dayton (513) 276-5961
Denver (303) 287-0381
Detroit (313) 547-9000
Hartford (203) 529-6861
Honolulu (808) 682-2020
Houston (713) 672-1621
Indianapolis (317) 841-0033
Kansas City (816) 842-7300
Los Angeles (213) 567-1122
Minneapolis (612) 784-5000
Oakland (415) 835-8222
Philadelphia (215) 949-2850
Phoenix (602) 272-0461
St. Louis (314) 291-6080
Seattle (206) 762-4400
Tulsa (918) 835-1511

Joseph T. Ryerson & Son, Inc.
(a subsidiary of Inland Steel Industries, Inc.)
Boston (617) 782-6900
Buffalo (716) 894-3311
Charlotte (704) 392-1321
Chattanooga (615) 499-3500
Chicago (312) 762-2121
Cincinnati (513) 542-5800
Cleveland (216) 432-1411
Dallas (214) 637-4710
Denver (303) 287-0101
Des Moines (615) 262-5151
Detroit (313) 874-3311
Houston (713) 675-6111
Indianapolis (317) 359-8282
Jersey City (201) 435-3434
Kansas City (816) 471-3500
Los Angeles (213) 268-7100
Milwaukee (414) 453-8000
Minneapolis (612) 544-4401
Omaha (402) 895-5056
Philadelphia (215) 724-0700
Phoenix (602) 233-6100
Pittsburgh (412) 276-5400
Portland (503) 285-4611
Salt Lake City (801) 773-0421
San Francisco (510) 653-2933
Seattle (206) 624-2300
Spokane (509) 535-1581
St. Louis (314) 231-1020
Tulsa (918) 428-3841
Wallingford (203) 269-8744

Wisconsin Steel and Tube Corporation
1555 North Mayfair Road, P.O. Box 26365
Milwaukee, WI 53226
(414) 453-4441, (800) 279-9335, FAX (414) 453-0789

Footnotes

1 Copyright © *Thomas Register of American Manufacturers*, 83rd ed., Vol. 14, 1993, Thomas Publishing Company, New York, NY.

2 U.S. Bureau of Mines, Mineral Commodity Summaries, January 1994.

3 Excludes U. S. production.

4 American Purchasing Society, 1992 estimates.

CHAPTER 7

Background for Nonferrous Metal Purchasing

The chemical names for materials that contain iron include the words ferrous or ferric; for example, ferrous oxide and ferric oxide have the chemical symbols FeO and Fe_2O_3, respectively. That may clarify why metals that do not contain iron are called nonferrous. The nonferrous metal industries are those involved with the mining, refining, and production of metal substances other than those that contain iron.

There are many such metals in the list of elements, but relatively few have major significance for most uses. However, alloys of those metals that are used widely may contain small amounts of the other less important metals. Other than iron and steel, the most used metals are aluminum, copper, and zinc.

Aluminum

Pure aluminum is a lightweight, silvery colored element with the chemical symbol Al. It has an atomic number of 13[1], an atomic weight of 26.9815, and a melting point of 659°C (1218.2° F). It is corrosion resistant except for a transparent film that appears on the surface that is exposed to air or oxygen. Once this film of aluminum oxide develops, it goes no further into the metal, but rather protects the metal from further corrosion.

Aluminum is the most abundant metal in the earth's crust. The nonmetals oxygen and silicon are the only elements more plentiful. However, aluminum is never found in its pure state; and most ores, such as aluminum

91

silicate, are expensive to use to extract the metal. The ore used in the United States to obtain aluminum is called bauxite. Usually it is obtained from open pit mines, but deeper mines using shafts and tunnels are also sometimes used. It is found and mined all over the world. According to the U.S. Bureau of Mines, "Bauxite resources (reserves plus subeconomic and undiscovered deposits) are estimated to be 55 – 75 billion tons, located in South America (33%), Africa (27%), Asia (17%), Oceania (13%), and elsewhere (10%). Domestic resources of bauxite are inadequate to meet long-term demand, but the United States and most other major aluminum-producing countries have essentially inexhaustible subeconomic resources of aluminum in materials other than bauxite."

"Bauxite is the only raw material used in the production of alumina (aluminum oxide) on a commercial scale in the United States. However, the vast U.S. resources of clay are technically feasible sources of alumina. Other domestic raw materials, such as anorthosite, alunite, coal wastes, and oil shales, offer additional potential alumina sources."[2]

1993 WORLD ALUMINUM SMELTER PRODUCTION AND CAPACITY (IN THOUSANDS OF METRIC TONS)

Location	Production	Year-End Capacity
United States	3,700	4,163
Australia	1,350	1,380
Azerbaijan	20	58
Brazil	1,170	1,196
Canada	2,200	2,265
France	450	472
Russia	2,700	2,970
Tajikistan	300	517
Ukraine	80	110
Venezuela	570	640
Other Countries	6,460	8,266
World Total	19,000	22,037

Source: Mineral Commodity Summaries, 1994, U.S. Bureau of Mines

History and Development

Aluminum is one of the most recent metals to be commercially refined and used. Although alum, an aluminum compound, was used several thousand years ago, the existence of the metal itself was only discovered in 1746, and it was not isolated until 1825. It was not until 1845 that a German chemist, Friedrich Wholer, was able to reproduce a few drops of aluminum. The Emperor Napoleon III wanted to use aluminum for military equipment, but only a few tons could be produced annually until a new process was separately and almost simultaneously invented in 1886 by Charles Martin Hall in the United States and Paul-Louis-Toussaint Heroult in France. The method, referred to as the Hall – Heroult process, is the electrolytic reduction of purified alumina.

The raw material, alumina, is obtained from bauxite by using either the Bayer process or the Alcoa combination process. The Bayer process is used to obtain alumina from a good grade of bauxite. It involves drying, grinding, and placing the bauxite under pressure in a solution of sodium hydroxide. The alumina dissolves in the solution, and the undissolved silica and other impurities are removed by filtration. The final steps require precipitation of the sodium aluminate to obtain aluminum hydroxide crystals which are then heated to obtain aluminum oxide. The Alcoa combination process is used when a lower grade of bauxite is refined. It involves recycling the "red mud" or waste material produced in the Bayer process.

Uses of Aluminum

In addition to the packaging industry — for such items as cans and foil — aluminum is used extensively in the manufacture of airplanes, automobiles, and construction. It is particularly useful where the desired characteristic of light weight and strength are needed. As the importance of energy-saving devices has increased, so too has the demand for aluminum. For example, more aluminum is used in automobiles, because by reducing the weight of automobiles, gasoline consumption decreases. Aluminum wheels, wheel covers, engines, engine parts, and many other automobile and truck parts have replaced steel or cast iron in various models. The U.S. Bureau of Mines estimates that 33% of aluminum is used for packaging, 23% for transportation equipment, 17% for construction, 9% for electrical, 8% for consumer durables, and 10% for other uses.[3]

Although pure aluminum loses its strength when heated, alloys can withstand high or low temperatures. Aluminum is also used in construction, and is used to make cookware. Because of its excellent electrical conductivity and resistance to corrosion, it is also used for electrical applications.

Primary Aluminum Metal Pricing and Negotiations

Between 1989 and 1993, the average U.S. spot price of aluminum ingot declined from 87.8 cents per pound to 53.0 cents per pound. As a result, many producers temporarily closed their plants and reduced production to the lowest level in six years. The average price in 1992 was 57 cents per pound, in 1993 was 52 cents per pound, and in 1994 was 67 cents per pound. In early May 1994, the price was 61.5 cents per pound. The LME cash price was 89 cents per pound by December 31. On May 2, 1995, the price closed at 90.9 cents per pound.

Those prices printed in magazines, newspapers, and announced by the suppliers should only be used as a guide by buyers. Sometimes any particular buyer will be able to purchase material at lower prices than those sources show, and sometimes a buyer will pay more. It depends on what is really going on in the marketplace, how much the buyer is going to buy, and relationships with the suppliers. The purchasing company's payment record, financial stability, and how the products are going to be used are all factors. Perhaps the single most important variable is the ability of the buyer to negotiate.

The smart buyer knows that announced prices from suppliers don't always hold up. Many times, industry-announced price increases are rescinded because of general buyer resistance to those increases.

A word about published lead times is also appropriate. The lead times printed in magazines may be obtained from buyers or sellers who overestimate the normal amount of time to receive material. In the author's experience, the actual amount of time between placing an order and the receipt of goods is usually less than what appears in the press.

Aluminum Fabrications

Pure aluminum softens at elevated temperatures and hardens when it is cool. It is easy to work hardened aluminum as well. Aluminum or aluminum alloys can be cast, forged, extruded, die cast, rolled, stamped, or drawn. Aluminum extrusions are made by forcing the metal through a die of the desired shape. Long lengths of moldings or strips for construction and architectural uses are made in this way. The long extrusions are cut to the desired shorter lengths.

Aluminum die castings are made by melting the raw metal and injecting it into the mold. The mold separates and ejects the hardened cooling metal. Both zinc and aluminum are commonly used metals in making die castings.

Pricing and Negotiations on Fabricated Aluminum and Aluminum Alloys

Published primary metal prices are often used as a guide in determining a fair price for a product made of the same material. If the price of the primary metal rises or falls, the buyer should expect similar moves in price in the fabrication. However, the picture is clouded somewhat because fabricated items are more often than not made out of alloys. Price movements for those alloys do not always correspond to the price movements of the primary metal. The producers sometimes leave the price of the alloy alone or even increase it when the price of the pure metal is being decreased. The buyer should not be entirely daunted by this. With sufficient negotiating power and skill, the supplier may accept reasonable arguments in favor of the buyer's position.

Copper

Copper has the chemical symbol Cu, the atomic number 29, atomic weight 63.54, and the melting point of 1083°C (1981°F). Copper is frequently referred to as the "red" metal, since it has a somewhat reddish to gold color. It is one of the oldest metals used by man, going far back into prehistoric times. Today it is still widely used and of paramount importance in the life of civilized society. Because of its properties, it has many uses, 42% for building construction, 24% for electrical and electronic products, 13% for industrial machinery and equipment, 11% for transportation equipment, and 10% for general products.[4]

Compounds of copper usually have the name cuprous, in which the copper has a valence of one; or cupric with a valence of two. In addition to the uses of the pure metal or metal alloys, cupric compounds are used in (or used to make) various products such as paint, insecticides, and fungicides.

Copper has high electric conductivity. It is relatively corrosive resistant, and is easy to work. It can be drawn into fine wire because of its high degree of ductility.

1993 WORLD MINE PRODUCTION AND RESERVES OF COPPER [5] (IN THOUSANDS OF METRIC TONS)

Location	Production	Reserves[6]
United States	1,770	45,000
Australia	300	7,000
Canada	750	11,000
Chile	2,020	88,000
China	380	3,000
Indonesia	270	11,000
Peru	370	7,000
Philippines	130	7,000
Poland	390	20,000
U.S.S.R.[7]	800	37,000
Zaire	90	10,000
Zambia	420	12,000
Other countries	1,590	50,000
World Total	9,300	310,000

Methods of Refining Copper

There are several methods of refining copper depending on the raw material used; but the process of refining the ore and purifying the copper involves a number of steps before the copper is used by industrial fabricators. Because copper ore only contains a small percentage of copper, the ore must be concentrated before smelting in order to make it economical. The ore is crushed into a fine powder or concentrate. A froth or chemical flotation process is used wherein the fine material is treated with a "collector" or "promoter" to make the copper-bearing material adhere to bubbles that float to the surface and become a froth.

The froth containing concentrate is skimmed off, and after drying is roasted to remove unwanted oxides and excessive amounts of sulfur. The material is then smelted in a reverberatory matte furnace.

Copper Pricing

Copper prices, as is true of all prices, are dependent on supply and demand; but the supply of metal ores and other natural products is a function of readily available high-quality ores, known reserves of low-grade ores, and estimates of yet undiscovered deposits. Demand is affected by the availability and cost of substitute products. Thus far, the need for copper in the foreseeable future is well established, and the International Trade Administration of the U.S. Department of Commerce estimates demand to increase in the United States by a compound rate of 1.5% – 1.7% annually, and by 2% worldwide through the year 2000.[8] Copper purchasers include investors and speculators who buy and sell the commodity through the London Metal Exchange (LME) and the New York Commodity Exchange (COMEX). Prices reported in these markets, to a large extent, reflect the current demand of copper and copper products. It is very helpful for the buyer of copper and copper products to check the prices from these exchanges which are printed daily in *The Wall Street Journal*. Prices are given for the spot or cash market and the futures market. For example, the closing spot price for high-grade copper on May 3, 1995 on the COMEX, as reported in *The Wall Street Journal*, was $1.27 per pound, and the three month forward price for copper cathode on the LME was $2733 per metric ton. Since there is a well-established market for copper futures, a buyer can use hedging methods to provide assurance that the price paid for a copper product will not turn out to be excessive because of changes in the market. The following section describes how hedging may be used.

Hedging to Reduce Risk

One or more of the commodity exchanges deals in aluminum, tin, copper, gold, lead, mercury, nickel, silver, zinc, and various other precious metals. Buyers of metal and products containing metals, such as copper, brass, and bronze, may buy future contracts on the commodity exchanges to make certain that changes in the price they pay will not seriously affect profits. The broker is paid a commission which is a small percentage of the buy or sell transaction.

For example, suppose you want to buy 100,000 pounds of copper to use to make the product you sell, and the price is $1.07 per pound. You do not want to gamble that the price of copper will fall during the manufacturing process and reduce the price that your product will sell for. Therefore, you sell the same amount of copper today for delivery at a future date. If the price of copper rises to $1.20, you would lose on the sale of the future contract, but at the same time your copper product becomes more valuable. You sell your copper or copper product at an additional profit of 13 cents per pound and use the proceeds to buy enough copper to make delivery or cover the short sale.

On the other hand, suppose that instead of the copper going up in price it goes down to 94 cents per pound. Since you sold a futures contract at $1.07, you make a profit of 13 cents per pound on the futures sale even though you lose on the cost of the product you make.

Brass

Brass is a commonly used alloy of copper. Although there are different types of brasses, they generally contain from 5 to about 45 percent zinc along with the copper, which makes the metal harder as well as ductile and malleable. When brass is under internal stress, cracks along the grain boundaries sometimes occur. Keeping the zinc content low or annealing will help prevent this condition.

Another problem with brass is that it may corrode and thereby lose its zinc content. The addition of aluminum or tin to the alloy will help prevent corrosion, but both reduce ductility. Various other additives produce alloys that provide advantages for particular applications. However, there are usually tradeoffs — i.e., with every advantage there are disadvantages, even if these only involve a higher monetary price; a certain disadvantage may not matter for the application intended.

Formerly, copper with tin was called brass, but we now refer to that combination as bronze.

Bronze

Bronze is an alloy of copper with various elements such as aluminum, beryllium, silicon, and tin. Bronze is stronger and harder than other common alloys except steel. It is better than steel in resisting corrosion.

Other Copper Alloys

Nickel is combined with copper for applications requiring high strength and corrosion resistance. A combination of copper, nickel, and zinc is used for items requiring good mechanical properties and corrosion resistance. Such material is referred to as nickel silver or German silver. It is used to make various items such as hardware and drawing instruments. The metal also acts as a base material for plating.

Monel alloys contain a high percentage of nickel with the copper and various small amounts of other elements. These alloys are used where resistance to chemical reaction is important

Pricing of Copper Alloys and Copper Products

One of the best ways to check prices on any product is to shop and ask for bids from available sources. Of course, this works best when there is more competition rather than less. Another way to check prices is to use the published figures from the commodity markets. You can't use the commodity markets directly to find out the current prices of alloys and fabricated products because alloys and fabricated products are not traded. However, if you know the constituents of the alloy or how much metal is in the fabricated product, you can estimate what the price should be, or at least determine the direction the price is moving. For example, if you buy a fabricated item that sells for $50, and it is made of a certain alloy that contains 95% copper, you can begin to estimate what the price will be. Let us say that the part weighs 10 pounds. The COMEX price of copper is at $1.05 per pound. Then copper goes up to $1.20 per pound. How much more will you have to pay for your item? You then calculate that 95% of the material cost of your item was $1.05 X 10 pounds = $10.50. Let us further assume that the alloy was a brass with 5% zinc. Zinc is selling at 56.3 cents per pound. The part contains 5% of the 10 pounds of zinc or one-half pound of zinc worth 26 cents. Thus, the total cost of the material is about $10.76. Now assume the price of zinc stays the same, but the price of copper goes up to $1.20. Then the 15 cents per pound price of copper is a 14.3% rise in our copper content or 0.143 X $10.50 = $1.50. This is a very rough estimate since the cost of any particular alloy may be very different than the constituents. Nevertheless, it is a guide; because you know if any of the component's costs are changing, the total will also change. Sometimes the price will go up and sometimes it will go down. Keep in mind that you need to look at all of the component costs — not just one or two, because one could offset another.

If the item is a common easy-to-make alloy, the aggregated costs of the components will be closer to the total alloy cost. If the alloy is difficult and therefore more costly to make, the aggregated costs of the components will fall short of the cost of the alloy.

Additional factors are the channel of distribution and the quantity purchased. Large quantities directly from the mill will cost less and be closer to the prices reported on the exchanges. The direction of the price movements and the approximate percentages should usually be the same unless there are extenuating circumstances. The buyer's negotiating ability may end up being the deciding factor on what price is paid.

Pricing of Fabricated Items

When calculating or estimating prices for fabricated items, the above methods may also be used; but, in addition, factors are added for labor, the cost of the equipment used, and burden. The buyer should try to shop for fabricated items to determine competitive prices. Be aware that fabricators will often bid higher when they have plenty of work and a large backlog of orders.

Sources for Nonferrous Metals

ASARCO Incorporated
180 Maiden Lane
New York, NY 10038
(212) 510-2000

ASARCO produces copper, lead, zinc, and silver from its own mines and from Southern Peru Copper Corporation, in which it has a 53% interest. It is one of the world's leading producers of nonferrous metals. According to the company, it produces about 13% of the Western World's mine production of copper, 12% of silver, 19% of lead, and 9% of zinc. Sales of products and services for 1994 were $2031.8 million. Of that, $1675 million were for metals, $278 million was for specialty chemicals, $43 million was for aggregates, and $36 million was for other products. The company has 8000 employees.

Alcan Aluminium Limited
1188 Sherbrooke Street West
P.O. Box 6090
Montreal, P.Q. , Canada H3C 3A7
(514) 848-8000
Telecopier (514) 848-8115

Established 93 years ago, Alcan Aluminium Limited is a major international company specializing in the mining of bauxite, refining alumina, and smelting aluminum. Alcan shipped 1952 thousand metric tons of fabricated product in 1994. It shipped 897 thousand metric tons of ingot, and produced 1435 thousand metric tons of aluminum during the same period. It also produced 496 thousand metric tons of secondary or recycled aluminum. In 1994, sales and operating revenues were $8216 million. It has 11 bauxite mines in 6 countries, 12 alumina plants in 9 countries, 13 smelters in 4 countries, 8 recycling plants in 4 countries, and over 100 manufacturing plants in 11 countries. The company employs approximately 37,500 people.

Aluminum Company of America Incorporated
1501 Alcoa Building
Pittsburgh, PA 15219
(412) 553-4545 FAX (412) 553-4498 Telex: 866470

Aluminum Company of America, known as Alcoa, is the world's leading producer of aluminum and alumina. It serves the packaging, automotive, aerospace, construction, and other markets with a variety of fabricated and finished products. In 1994, the company produced 655,000 metric tons of primary aluminum and 1,896,000 metric tons of fabricated finished aluminum products. The company has 22 business units with 169 facilities in 26 countries. In 1994, revenues were $9904.3 million and the average number of employees was 61,700.

Alumax Inc.
5655 Peachtree Parkway
Norcross, GA 30092-2812
(404) 246-6600

Alumax has five plants in North America, with capacity to produce 773,000 metric tons of aluminum. The company produces T-ingot and various alloy items. In 1995, it plans to expand its foil manufacturing operation which is the oldest in the United States. The company produces nonheat-treatable aluminum sheet and cast plate as well as aluminum extrusions and forgings. The company ships 35% of its product to distributors; 14% to the transportation industry; 11% for the packaging and container market; 10% for building construction; 9% for convertors, electrical, and other markets; 3% for machinery and equipment; and 8% for export. Net sales for 1994 were $2754.5 million and the company had 14,142 employees.

Cyprus Amax Minerals Company
9100 East Mineral Circle
Englewood, CO 80112
(303) 643-5000 Telex 216190 CMCO UR

Cyprus Amax Minerals mines and processes copper, molybdenum, coal, lithium, and gold internationally. In 1994, it produced 648 million pounds of copper. It has a workforce of 9500 people. Revenue in 1994 was $2788 million.

Inco Limited
Principal Executive Office
Royal Trust Tower
Toronto-Dominion Centre
Toronto, Ont. MSK1Ne Canada
(416) 361-7511

(Other Executive Office)
One New York Plaza
New York, NY 10004
(212) 612-5500

Inco has operating units and sales offices in locations all over the world. It is one of the world's leading mining and metals companies. It is a major producer of nickel — a hard, malleable metal used in thousands of products. In 1994, it delivered 517,660 pounds of nickel. It is an important producer of copper, precious metals, and cobalt. In 1994, it delivered 231,130 pounds of copper, including copper in alloys; and it delivered 2875 pounds of cobalt, 1170 troy ounces of silver, and 485 metric tons of sulfuric acid and liquid sulphur dioxide. During the same period, it delivered 111 troy ounces of platinum, 126 troy ounces of palladium, 11 troy ounces of rhodium, and 39 troy ounces of gold. Total net sales were $2484 millions. It has 15,709 employees in 21 countries.

Phelps Dodge Corporation
2600 North Central Avenue
Phoenix, AZ 85004-3014
(602) 234-8100

During 1994, Phelps Dodge and its associated companies produced 693.2 thousand tons of copper. In 1994, the company and its associated companies also produced 93 thousand ounces of gold, 1627 ounces of silver, 99 thousand pounds of molybdenum, and 1276.7 thousand tons of sulfuric acid. After seven years of exploration and development, the company began production of copper in 1994 from its new mining facility at the Candelaria deposit discovered in 1987. This facility, located in Chile's Atacam Desert, will increase the company's annual production by 20%. In 1994, the company had revenue of $3289.2 million. Of that amount, 55.4% came from Phelps Dodge Mining which includes mining, refining, and casting of copper. The balance of 44.6% came from Phelps Dodge Industries which includes companies that produce rims for trucks, trailers, and buses; carbon blacks and synthetic iron oxides; magnet wire; electrical and telecommunications cables; and specialty high-performance conductors. In 1994, ISO 9000 certification upgrades were obtained by the El Paso and Norwich Rod Plants. ISO certifications were acquired by two Phelps Dodge Magnet Wire facilities and six facilities of Phelps Dodge International Corporation. Phelps Dodge Corporation has 15,000 employees in 15 countries.

Reynolds Metals Company
6601 West Broad Street
Richmond, VA 23230
(804) 281-2000

Annual sales for Reynolds Metals in 1994 were $6013.2 million and net income was $121.7 million. The company employed 29,000 people. The company began operations 75 years ago in Louisville, KY, as the U.S. Foil Company. Reynolds and its affiliates now operate more than 100 manufacturing facilities in 22 countries; 7% of its revenue comes from the production of primary aluminum, and 69% from fabricated aluminum products. The balance of 24% is from nonaluminum products.

In 1994, packaging and containers accounted for 45% of revenue, distributors and fabricators accounted for 13%, building and construction for another 13%, automotive and transportation 12%, and electrical 3%. The balance of 14% was attributable to other markets.

Examples of specific products made by Reynolds include the all-aluminum wheels on the Chrysler LHS luxury sedan, and hoods for the 1995 Buick Riviera and Lincoln Town Car; Reynolds Wrap for household foil; aluminum cans for beer, soft drinks, and juices; and fabricated aluminum products for bridges.

Kennecott Corporation
10 East South Temple, P.O. Box 11248
Salt Lake City, UT 84147
(801) 322-8295

All of Kennecott common stock is owned by The RTZ Corporation PLC, a British-based company that employs 44,499 people worldwide in the mining and metal industries. RTZ mines supply 7 percent of the world's copper. RTZ also produces gold, iron ore, aluminum, zinc, lead silver, coal, borax, uranium, and other metals and mined products.

Sources for Further Information

Industry Associations

Aluminum Association
900 19th Street, N.W.
Washington, DC 20006
(202) 862-5100 FAX (202) 862-5164

Copper Development Association, Inc.
260 Madison Avenue
New York, NY 10016
(212) 251-7200 FAX (212) 251-7234

Publications

U.S. Industrial Outlook is published annually by the U.S. Department of Commerce, International Trade Administration. It may be ordered from the Superintendent of Documents, P.O. Box 371954, Pittsburgh, PA 15250-7954. Price as of this writing is $37, or $46.25 foreign.

Mineral Commodity Summaries is published by the U. S. Department of the Interior, Bureau of Mines. Order from the Superintendent of Documents, U.S. Government Printing Office, Washington, DC.

Footnotes

[1] The atomic number represents the number of electrons in an element's atom.

[2] Mineral Commodity Summaries, 1994, United States Department of the Interior, Bureau of Mines.

[3] Mineral Commodity Summaries, 1994, United States Department of the Interior, Bureau of Mines.

[4] Mineral Commodity Summaries, 1994, United States Department of the Interior, Bureau of Mines.

[5] Mineral Commodity Summaries, 1994, United States Department of the Interior, Bureau of Mines.

[6] Reserves are the part of the reserve base which could be economically extracted or produced at the time of determination.

[7] As constituted before December 1991.

[8] U.S. Industrial Outlook, 1994, U.S. Department of Commerce, International Trade Administration.

CHAPTER 8

Important Differences in Buying Fabricated Metal Items

As mentioned earlier, the buyer receives the requisition from the user or from an engineering function that provides detailed specifications on the item that needs to be purchased. In some cases, especially when there is no formal purchasing operation, the engineer or user is also the buyer. Regardless of the case, the person assigned the job of selecting potential suppliers, negotiating the best agreement, and documenting the transaction must do more than accept a requisition, drawing, or other specification, and then place the order without question. However, questioning the need for a product must be handled with extreme delicacy and diplomacy. Many buyers limit these types of questions because they do not feel it is their responsibility or right to question the needs of users. Such questioning should never be done just to show or exert power or authority, but strictly to offer suggestions for alternative ways of obtaining the products or services that the users want. For example, a buyer may know of raw material that is available from another plant or from another department and so can avoid spending money on a product from an outside source. The buyer may suggest using alternate surplus material that may have slightly different specifications that will more than satisfy the needs of the user.

Other types of questions may actually change the specifications and satisfy the user's needs. In more cases than not, specification changes may not be made on the immediate requirements. They will usually be made on later requirements after approval by engineering, marketing, quality control, or various other departments within the organization. For example, inventory control may object to changing specifications on an item until quantities of other older stocked items that will be affected are used up or substantially reduced.

The adequately trained buyer is often able to see the advantages of changing specifications that may radically alter the product or change the source of supply and thereby provide substantial cost reductions. Cost reductions may come in a number of different ways such as in the form of a reduced purchase price, or in the requirement of less internal labor for manufacturing. Savings may be obtained by lower transportation cost or a better quality product.

One might ask why the user or engineer does not produce the best or most appropriate specification the first time? Why would any change be necessary? To answer this question, it is necessary to understand the motivation and goals of the user or engineer. Normally, users and engineers are primarily concerned with producing a usable product. They are concerned that the product will work or perform the function intended, and that it will be trouble free. Usually, they are working under time constraints, and they are concerned that the product is produced in time to meet schedules. While they would certainly claim that they are also concerned with cost (and deny any allegations to the contrary), cost considerations are not their highest priority. In addition, engineers and other requestors have little or no knowledge of the marketplace. They seldom have extensive contact outside the organization where they work. The reverse is true of the buyer, who is primarily concerned about cost. The buyer has a better chance to see what alternatives are available in the marketplace.

The buyer must obtain a product that works and must have it delivered on time. If he or she obtains the item as requested by the user from a reputable source of supply — and does nothing else — then any failure of the product is attributable to the requestor. After all, the buyer bought what was requested, and the supplier delivered what was requested. Thus, if a buyer wants to "play it safe," the best course of action is to simply buy the item requested. But the competent and conscientious buyer will do much more than that. If the design calls for a stamping, but it will be more economical to have a casting, the buyer will obtain bids from casting suppliers.

The only way that a buyer can know if it is worthwhile to obtain such bids is to understand the advantages and disadvantages of different types of products, and to understand how the purchased item is to be used. What follows is a description of various ways of making products and the advantages and disadvantages of each. With this knowledge, a buyer may recommend changes or obtain bids to determine if another type of process might lower cost or improve performance.

Forgings

Many years ago, I was Purchasing Agent for Forgings at the Automotive Division of North American Rockwell (now Rockwell International). My responsibilities included buying from hundreds of outside forging companies in addition to conducting internal transactions concerned with Rockwell's own forging plant in Detroit. The thousands of items purchased were iron or steel forgings of various sizes ranging from parts that could be held in the hand to those as big as a desk. Most of the items were for trucks and military vehicles such as half-tracks and tanks. Quantities ranged from a few pieces to several thousand. Rockwell provided drawings, but many of the specifications were established by the military.

At that time, Rockwell had separate purchasing departments at various locations in different states. Part of my job, and that of other purchasing agents in our office, was to centralize the buying operation, that is, bring all the records from each branch location to our office and make the purchases for each of those plants from our office.

What I was astounded to discover was that many of the local Rockwell plants were paying different prices for exactly the same forging from the same supplier. In some cases, the prices were significantly different. This is a clear indication of the importance of negotiating effectively (it is also a good example of one of the advantages of centralized purchasing). We never tabulated the potential loss of profit as a result of these different prices, but it was probably substantial.

How Forgings Are Made

The first thing a new buyer of metal fabrications needs to learn is what forgings are and how they are made. Forgings are parts that are shaped out of metal by hammering, impacting, or pressing the raw metal material. Hammering metal is one of the oldest metal-working processes, going back several thousand years. The smith or blacksmith shop was a forging operation. Forged items are made by either using hot raw material that is above the recrystallization temperature, or by using cold raw material below the recrystallization temperature. The finished product has a high degree of

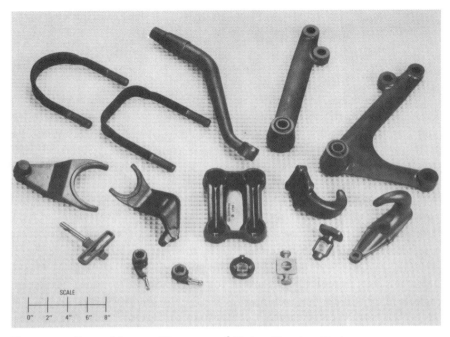

Figure 8-1. Forged items. (Courtesy of Union Forging Co.)

strength as a result of the forces used to shape the product. Pounding the metal creates stresses in the metal. The metal has a grain structure or pattern aligned in a certain direction and reflecting the forces. The forging process traditionally is used for very strong, tough, metal parts. Similar items can be produced by casting, or sometimes by using metal forms that are welded or fastened together. However, although a casting may be less expensive because it is less labor intensive, it usually is not as strong and is prone to quality problems. Because of advances in metallurgy, casting quality and reliability are now much better than they once were, but it all depends on whom you talk to. Casting suppliers will stress the advantages of castings; forging suppliers will emphasize the benefits of using forgings. Poorly produced castings will contain air bubbles or voids that make the metal weak. The outward appearance does not always show this weakness. It takes an X-ray to reveal problems. Sometimes porosity is discovered during or after many wasted hours of machining. In all likelihood, the item must then be scrapped. On the other hand, it may be much more difficult to machine forgings because of their extreme toughness.

In most cases, the most economical choice between making an item from either a forging or a casting largely depends on the final use of the product. If you want ultimate strength, a forging is probably your choice. However, it is not quite that simple. Changing the configuration or geometry of the part affects the cost as well as the choice of raw material. The shape of the item may preclude using a forging unless extensive machining is done after the forging is made. On the other hand, metal will flow into complex openings to make a casting to fit the purpose intended. If the finish on a part is not important, high strength is needed, and the configuration is not too complex, a forging is probably the best choice.

Items made from forgings can range from very small parts weighing only a few ounces to large items weighing more than 150 tons. Forgings are often divided into various types related to how they are manufactured. They include impression die forgings, open die forgings, seamless rolled rings, and cold forgings. Impression die forgings, usually referred to as closed die forgings, are made by using dies that are dropped or pressed together to force the metal into the configuration of the die. As the die is closed, some metal is forced between the top and bottom die. This material is called flash. The parting line or flash can be clearly detected on a forged item if it has not been machined off.

Drop hammers operate vertically by gravity at the rate of 14 feet per second; by using steam and air pressure, the rate of travel increases to about 30 feet per second.

Horizontal forging machines, called upsetters, also use dies. One die remains fixed and the other moves up and down to hold the material in place or release it while a "header tool" exerts pressure from the side.

The Forging Industry Association lists 130 members with over 175 forging plants. The suppliers for impression die forgings have gravity hammer equipment ranging in size from 500 to 12,000 pounds. Power hammers range in size from 1000 to 50,000 pounds. Mechanical presses range in size from 1 ton to 12,000 tons. Hydraulic presses range in size from 20 tons to 55,000 tons. Upsetters range in size from 1 inch to 10 inches.

The Forging Industry Association claims that their members account for 65% of the forgings produced in the United States and Canada.

Stampings

Thousands of products are made by stamping out a desired shape from a variety of materials such as steel, aluminum, and copper. The raw mater-

Figure 8-2. Stamping presses. (Courtesy of the Minster Machine Co.)

ial can be thick or thin; relatively hard or soft; simple, common, and inexpensive; or specially produced and very expensive. Low carbon steel or costly stainless steel with a high degree of corrosion resistance can be used. The material may be coated, galvanized, or clad. Stampings are used to make automobile and truck bodies, appliances, cookware, garden tools, and a myriad of other products with a myriad of uses.

How Stampings Are Made

Stampings are produced by punching or pressing the metal with dies to achieve the desired shape. Some of the dies are designed so that the metal is simply bent into a certain shape as a press-break machine brings force on the material that is pressed against the dies. The dies may be so designed that the machine will shear off or cut through the material producing holes of a desired shape. The waste material thus generated is transported in one direction away from the stamping machine by hand, gravity, automated mechanisms, or conveyors. The desired finished item is moved in another direction by hand or conveyor to a storage container.

Sometimes, the raw material is worked by one set of dies, automatically or manually moved, worked by another set of dies and moved again to a third set of dies. In this way, very complex shapes can be obtained with two or three bends or cutouts or combinations of bends and cutouts.

The designer of a stamping tries to use the material in the most efficient manner possible, so that as many pieces of good items are produced out of a given size sheet or coil, and so that minimum scrap is generated. If possible, the slugs or punchouts are used as raw material to produce other items.

Raw material such as steel may be thin or thick. It may be in the form of sheets that are fed into the machine manually, or it may be a continuous coil. New coils are placed on large reels, and once started the material is unwound and fed into the stamping machine automatically. The type of machine needed will depend on the thickness of the material and the number of pieces to be produced. It requires less force to produce a stamping from thin material, and therefore a small or less powerful machine is necessary. A more complex machine is required for an automated process, whereas a simpler press-break will do the job if the material is to be fed by hand.

All of these factors affect the price of the product, and the buyer should be aware of them to understand one reason why costs may vary between sources.

Where to Source

There are hundreds (if not thousands) of companies that produce stampings. Many make the items for their own use as a normal step in their manufacturing process. The buyer should consider the pros and cons of obtaining equipment necessary to meet stamping requirements internally. The costs of setting up your own stamping operation are significant and must be carefully weighed. Many factors should be evaluated.

Are stampings required for products that will be produced for many years to come? If this question cannot be answered unequivocally and emphatically "yes," then further consideration of making your own stampings is probably unnecessary. Why invest in costly equipment if it can't be amortized in the time needed?

But there are other questions that you need to answer. Is there available space to produce the product efficiently and economically? If not, can the space be obtained cheaply?

Perhaps the most important question of all concerns the availability of qualified personnel to design and produce the items required. Will you be able to hire trained and qualified people at reasonable wage rates to produce the quality you need? With so many outside sources available, no one should rush into producing their own stamping items. Many companies do have their own stamping operations as one stage of their manufacturing process. However, these companies are usually relatively large and make products that continually require the use of the stamping equipment.

Companies that make it their business to produce stampings for others vary in size from small shops (with only a few thousand square feet of operating space and a few dozen workers or less) to gigantic plants with hundreds of workers. The small shops tend to produce small items that require less expensive equipment; often they produce the items from sheets or strips that may be hand fed. The larger shops may also produce small items such as brackets or other small parts, but generally the machines are automated. In addition, the larger shops often produce parts from coils of material that are automatically fed into the presses.

Prices and Costs

The price of the parts produced is based on the usual factors such as material, labor, and overhead. Well-determined prices include a cost factor depending on which machine or machines are used to make the item. Most machines require set-up time before they begin producing items. Stamping dies need to be removed and new ones inserted, adjusted, and tested. The time taken to do this setup and produce the stampings is multiplied by the amortized cost of the machine. Thus, to take a hypothetical example, if a machine costs $500,000 and will be amortized over 10 years, the per-hour cost of that machine might be $28 per hour. If 2 hours of set-up were required to run a certain item, then $56 would be applied before the first piece was even run. If the quantity needed will take 10 hours to run, an additional $280 must be added. Add labor costs for 12 hours at $15 per hour, which is $180 for our example. Our subtotal is now up to $516. Let us say that the material cost is $1250. Our subtotal is now $1766, or $2649 with a 50% burden or overhead rate for the job without profit. Add 20% for profit, and the job is quoted at $3178.80. If this is for a quantity of 5000, then the piece price at this quantity is $0.6356 each.

If a machine that costs half as much to purchase is used, then the per hour amortized cost of that machine would be half as much. The buyer may

Figure 8-3. Stamped items. (Courtesy of Astron.)

be fortunate in having a supplier that has many sizes and types of machines. The supplier can put the job on one machine that carries double the cost of another. The supplier normally will not tell the buyer which machine the item will be run on or, for that matter, what the cost of each machine is. It is up to the buyer to dig that information out during negotiations.

Suppliers will be reluctant to give this information for several reasons. First, they may not be certain which machine they will use at any one time, and they don't want to restrict their ability to make decisions as they go along. Certain machines might be tied up with other customers at any one time.

Second, suppliers do not always measure their cost this way. They may use an average cost of all equipment. This could work to the advantage or disadvantage of the buyer, depending on the type of work you require. The most certain way to get cost information is to compare the bids of several suppliers and try to obtain information about the equipment that will be used to produce your requirements. Try to obtain as much detail about costs as possible. You can estimate any missing cost factors. These estimates are very useful when negotiating.

Another factor to consider is the size of the dies and whether they are adaptable to different types or sizes of equipment. If they will not fit or cannot easily be revised to fit a lower cost piece of equipment, then there is no use in worrying about this aspect of your sourcing decision.

Keep in mind that suppliers do not always know their true costs. Some will estimate their costs, and their bids will be based on those estimates. The result for the buyer is that many bids are unjustifiably high while others may be too low. Don't assume that you should always use those low bidders. It's great if the low bidder has the staying power to fill your orders and will be around when you need it. The danger is that bids below costs often result in poor quality, late deliveries, and other problems. Suppliers who suddenly realize they have been selling at a loss will try to escape from the contract by either asking for a much higher price or by simply not filling the order. Although the buyer may be in the right to demand that the order be filled as agreed, it is not always a certainty that he will win if the dispute is taken to court. Furthermore, suppliers that sell below costs can go out of business without much warning and leave the buyer scurrying around to find another source to meet schedules.

Forging Suppliers

Consolidated Industries, Inc.
Mixville Road
P.O. Box 280
Cheshire, CT 06410
(203) 272-5371 FAX (203) 272-5672

Consolidated Industries, Inc. has been supplying both ferrous and nonferrous alloy closed die forgings to the aerospace program since 1948. The items range in size from 1 ounce to 200 pounds. The plant has 100,000 square feet of floor space. The company's equipment includes hydraulic presses to 2500 ton mechanical presses to 1300 ton and steam hammers to 12,000 pounds capacity. It has trim presses to 400 ton and vertical and horizontal band saws. It has various heat treating and finishing capabilities.

EBC Industries
Erie Bolt Division
1325 Liberty Street
Erie, PA 16502
(814) 456-4287 FAX (814) 456-4280

EBC was founded in 1913. It produces forgings from raw material, and provides heat-treating and in-house machining and mechanical testing, specializes in fasteners, and has 105 employees.

Moline Forge
4101 Fourth Avenue
Moline, IL 61265
(309) 762-5506 FAX (309) 762-5508

Moline Forge was founded in 1915. The company is located in eight buildings with 80,000 square feet of manufacturing space. Equipment includes eleven drop hammers ranging in size from 2500 pounds to 8000 pounds. Trim presses range up to 200 tons capacity. The company has three Wheelabrators. Other equipment includes snag and air grinders, a 500 ton hydraulic coining press, and straightening presses from 40 to 75 tons. The company has sales volume of approximately $11 million, and employs 70 people. Customers include those in farm equipment manufacture, construction, off-highway equipment, railroad components, and recreational vehicles.

Queen City Forging Company
235 Tennyson Street
Cincinnati, OH 45226-1599
(513) 321-7200 FAX (513) 321-2004

Queen City Forging was started in 1881. Equipment includes drop hammers from 800 to 2000 pounds. Sales are below $5 million, and the company has 28 employees.

Teledyne Portland Forge
East Lafayette Street, P. O. Box 905
Portland, IN 47371-0905
(219) 726-8121 FAX (219) 726-8021

Teledyne Portland Forge has been in business since 1909. The company produces custom, impression die hot forgings of carbon and alloy steel for a multitude of industries. Equipment includes horizontal forging machines ranging in size from 3" to 8", and can form configurations up to 10" in diameter. Drop hammers range in size from 2000 to 10,000 pounds. The company produces long and short runs of items weighing from 1 pound to 200 pounds and uses over 150 different carbon and alloy steel grades. The company is owned by Teledyne, Inc., a large diversified corporation with head-

quarters in Los Angeles and eighteen operating companies. In 1994
Teledyne had sales of $2391.2 million.

Union Forging Company
500 North Street
Endicott, NY 13760
(607) 785-9975 FAX (607) 785-1927

Union Forging Company was started in 1883. It produces closed die
forgings in carbon, alloy, and stainless steels up to 50 pounds. Items produced include towing hooks and u-bolts. It uses gravity-type hammers ranging in size from 1000 to 5000 pounds. The company has its own tool room
with complete diemaking capabilities. It does annealing, normalizing, and
heat-quench-draw in-house.

Stamping Suppliers

Astron, Inc.
85 Northeastern Boulevard
Nashua, NH 03062
(603) 889-8500 FAX (603) 886-1543

Astron is a manufacturer of precision stampings. The company is a
result of the merger of Mass Machine and Stamping Co., a Boston company producing custom stampings and standard washers since 1905, and Dies
and Stampings, Inc., founded in Lowell, MA, in 1956. In 1975, operations
were moved to a new 45,000 square foot building where they are now located. Equipment includes presses ranging in size from 4 to 75 tons. The company reports that it has annual sales volume at $3.5 million and employs 30
people.

Checker Stamping & Mfg. Corp.
56-58 Elm Street
Newark, NJ 07105
(201) 589-3530 FAX (201) 589-4218

Checker began operation in 1955. It specializes in short run, small lot,
metal and plastic stampings. The company's equipment includes 22 presses
ranging in size from 3 ton to 98 tons, 5 press brakes, and 1 automatic shear
with 10 gauge capacity. The company is located in a 15,000 square foot fully
air conditioned building and has 18 employees. Reported annual sales are
$900,000.

Commercial Intertech
1775 Logan Avenue
Youngstown, OH 44501
(216) 746-8011 FAX (216) 746-1148 Telex 433-2153

Commercial Intertech produces medium to heavy stampings, tank heads, and pre-engineered steel building systems. It is an international organization with operations in twelve countries. Two U.S. plants produce tank heads and custom stampings for the agricultural, transportation, processing, mining, military, and industrial markets. It has five district sales offices and four distribution centers in the United States. Equipment at its Youngstown facility includes 38 presses ranging in size from 80 ton to 2000 ton capacity.

Industrial Dynamics Division
Industrial Components, Incorporated
P. O. Box 657
Davidson, NC 28036
(704) 892-0181 Telex 57-2399

Started in 1961, Industrial Dynamics produces custom high-speed stampings and assemblies. Facilities house 30 presses, from high-speed units up to 100 ton Minster automatics capable of producing parts in quantities from a handful to millions. The presses have automatic feed, variable speed, and electronic sensing devices. The company employs 20 people.

Industrial Spring Corporation
217 SW 33rd Court
Ft. Lauderdale, FL 33315
(305) 524-2558 FAX (305) 524-2550

Industrial Spring was started in 1969. It produces a wide variety of springs, wire forms, and light stampings. Quantities produced are from low to high volume. Tooling is supplied in-house. There are 12,000 square feet of manufacturing area and 17 employees.

KMC Stampings/KMC LaserForm Division
Kickhaefer Manufacturing Company
1221 S. Park Street, P.O. Box 348
Port Washington, WI 53074
(414) 284-3424 FAX (414) 284-9774

KMC started operations in 1908. It produces custom wire forms, stampings, and metal fabrications in both prototype and production quantities. Primary materials are carbon and stainless steel, brass, and aluminum. Annual sales are $18 million, and the company employs 100 people.

Morrissey, Inc.
9304 Bryant Avenue South
Bloomington, MN 55420
(612) 888-4675 FAX (612) 888-3915

Morrissey was started in 1946. It produces a wide range of custom stampings and assemblies in small to medium volumes. Sales volume ranges between $8.5 and $12.0 million and the company employs 75 people.

National Wire & Stamping, Inc.
2801 S. Vallejo Street
Englewood, CO 80110
(303) 762-8213 FAX (303) 777-9441

National Wire first began producing stampings and wire forms in 1959. The company occupies a modern 36,000 square foot plant incorporating design, prototype, testing, tooling and production capability under one roof. Equipment includes 22 fourslide and multislide machines, 15 punch presses, and 7 decoilers. Other equipment includes a wire forming machine, an injection molding machine, and a 55 ton press brake. Annual sales are about $5 million, and the company employs 35 people.

WEB Tool and Manufacturing, Inc.
1250 Greenleaf Avenue
Elk Grove Village, IL 60007
(708) 228-0105 FAX (708) 228-1792

WEB Tool and Manufacturing was established in 1980 as a privately owned tool and die shop, and expanded into metal stamping in 1984. It now has 26 presses ranging in size from 30 ton up to 350 ton.

Well Bilt Industries, Inc.
2 Maple Avenue
Linden, NJ 07036
(908) 846-2222 FAX (908) 486-2225

Well Bilt produces custom stampings up to a thickness of 0.25" from its 150 ton press. It makes items for the automotive, home appliance, electrical component, and housewares industries. The company has sales volume of $1.5 million, and employs 27 people.

For Further Information

Forging Industry Association
Landmark Office Towers
Suite 300-LTV
25 Prospect Avenue West
Cleveland, OH 44115
(216) 781-6260 FAX (216) 781-0102

The Forging Industry Association has various excellent publications available for buyers. The *1994–95 Custom Forging Capability Guide* explains the advantages of buying forgings, and lists its 130 member companies in North America, showing the size and type of equipment they have.

Precision Metalforming Association
27027 Chardon Road
Richmond Heights, OH 44143-1193
(216) 585-8800 FAX (216) 585-3126

Members of this organization include stampings companies, fabricators of metal, and suppliers of equipment to the metalforming industry. The Association publishes various guides, including a buyer's guide issue of its magazine, and a book of sources. There are approximately 1300 members.

Magazines

The Fabricator
The Croydon Group, Ltd.
833 Featherstone Road
Rockford, IL 61107-6302
(815) 399-8700 FAX (815) 399-7279

Metal Forming
PMA Services, Inc.
27027 Chardon Road
Richmond Heights, Ohio 44143-1193
(216) 585-8800 FAX (216) 585-3126

Directories

Buyer's Guide, 25th ed.
National Tooling & Machining Association
Ft. Washington, MD 20744
(301) 248-6200

CHAPTER 9

Select a Casting Source with Care

There are many types of castings and many types of processes that produce casting products. In most cases, the term "casting," when used by itself, usually applies to sand mold castings as opposed to die castings which are produced by forcing molten metal into a die.

Types of Casting Processes

Die Castings

Die castings made from aluminum, zinc, or other metals or alloys are produced by using machines that can produce high volumes of items quickly per mold. The items produced have a good finish and may have close tolerances. Unit cost is relatively low. Tooling cost is high, and the cost of maintaining tooling is high because of possible wear due to dies coming in direct contact with molten metal under pressure. Items produced are usually small because of the expensive machinery required, and the design is limited because any holes in the product must be tapered to allow for removal from the mold. The castings must go through an additional step to remove "flash" from the casting. Flash is the unwanted extra material that develops where the dies part.

Investment Casting

A very old method of producing castings sometimes is called the lost wax process, wherein a wax pattern is produced from a master die, which in turn is made from a master pattern. The wax pattern is used to make a mold and the wax is melted away.

Permanent Mold Castings

The permanent mold casting process also uses a reusable die and also produces an item with close tolerances and good surface finish, but high pressure is not used and the metal is gravity-fed into the mold. Bigger items can be produced than with regular die casting because simpler and less expensive equipment is used. Die cost is still relatively high. Higher temperatures may be used, allowing for use of various alloys not possible with regular die casting. Secondary operations are required to remove flash.

Sand Mold Castings

Sand mold castings are produced from iron, steel, alloys, or other metals by pouring molten metal into molds usually made of sand, although molds can be made from various other materials including graphite.

Different Types of Molds and Patterns

Some castings are referred to as "green sand castings." These are produced by using what is called green sand to make the mold. Green sand is a carefully selected and controlled sand that contains moisture. Molds may also be made of dry sand or various other materials. Each type of material or mold has advantages and disadvantages.

A skilled worker can make a mold by hand, but this is highly unusual in commercial production. In nearly all cases, a pattern is first produced to make the mold. Patterns may be made from pine, mahogany, aluminum, or polystyrene. The choice of one of these or other materials affects the pattern cost. However, the cost of the pattern is not the deciding factor in the total cost of producing a finished product. Pattern choice should be determined on the basis of dimensional tolerances needed, which casting or molding process will be used, required durability of the pattern, volume of product to be produced, the finish desired on the product, whether the finished product design is likely to remain the same or change, and the type of casting machinery that will be used.

The finished casting can never be better than the pattern it is made from. Therefore, it is very important to make certain that the pattern is properly made. Tolerances must be built into the pattern to allow shrinkage of the metal in the mold as the metal cools. Additional tolerances may be neces-

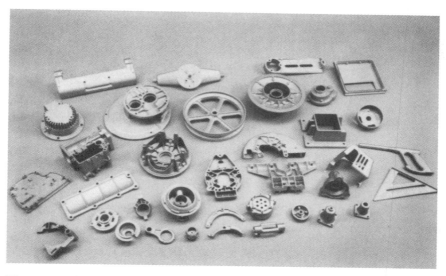

Figure 9-1. Cast items. (Courtesy of HBA Cast Products Company, Inc.)

sary if any secondary grinding or finishing operations need to be done on the castings.

In addition to the pattern and mold, cores or inserts are often required to produce castings. The metal flows between the core and the mold. Thus, the outside shape of the finished product is determined by the mold, and the inside shape is determined by the core. Cores are made in various ways depending on the design of the casting and the quantities needed. With small quantities, they are frequently made by packing sand containing a bonding agent into a "core box." The boxes are then turned over leaving the sand shapes on a tray. The sand is then baked. This produces cores that have sufficient strength to be placed in the mold and withstand the pressure of the metal poured around them. The heat from the metal destroys the bond and allows the sand to be easily removed from the hardened casting.

Use Care When Selecting a Casting Supplier

When you buy castings for the first time, it is especially important to choose the right source. That is because it can be more difficult to change sources than it is for other products not requiring tooling. However, choosing the right source is time consuming. You must make certain that you pick the source best qualified to make what you need.

Casting companies, or foundries as they are often called, frequently specialize in producing products made of a particular material or materials closely related. For example, some foundries specialize in steel castings, others produce products made of iron, others only produce aluminum items. Many produce various alloys of these elements or other metals.

Size is also a factor. There are foundries that are better suited to make castings from under 1 pound up to only a few pounds. Others can handle gigantic castings that weigh up to 100 tons. Some suppliers prefer small quantity runs and may not have the equipment to produce large quantities to meet schedules that may be required. Other companies do better with high volumes because they have the necessary facilities and equipment.

Many, if not most, suppliers will be honest with you, especially if you ask what they do best. If they can't produce what you want, some will suggest other sources that make what you need. But before deciding on any new supplier, it is best, if possible, to physically tour its operation. Observe what type of equipment is being used and what type of items are being produced.

Some foundries produce their own patterns, but many buy their patterns. As the buyer of the finished product, you may choose to buy the pattern yourself. However, if you do so, it is best to consult closely with the foundry that you are going to use, as patterns may not be suitable for the type of equipment they have. When you change casting sources and move your patterns from one foundry to another, it is sometimes necessary to incur the expense of revising the pattern to adapt to the new foundry. It may even be difficult for new sources to give you an accurate bid until they see the pattern you are using.

Traditionally, if it is likely that there will be repeat orders, foundries store patterns for their customers. Although foundries may not have the capabilities or desire to make patterns from scratch, many (if not most) have facilities to maintain or repair patterns. This service may be included in the price of the finished product, and the buyer should make sure who is responsible for maintenance and storage of the pattern. Before you choose a foundry, it is a good idea to inspect the storage area to see how well other customers' patterns are protected and whether they are identified. Make certain that the foundry has insurance covering any patterns that the foundry will keep for you. If you don't order castings on all your items regularly, it is a good idea to periodically inspect the patterns stored at the foundry. Make sure they are protected and being maintained properly. Even if you or the foundry has insurance, it can be very costly to discover that your patterns cannot be located or they are in poor condition when it comes time to use them.

Some casting companies have the capabilities to do secondary operations. If the castings are going to be machined, the foundry may be able to do the job at lower cost rather than having it shipped to another supplier.

Sometimes buyers will permit one supplier to subcontract a portion of the work to another supplier. For example, you may give an order to a machine shop to supply a finished casting requiring one or more machining operations. The machine shop is responsible to find the casting source, purchase the castings, and perform the necessary machining. Or you may contract with the casting company and allow them to have the work done by a machine shop. In either case, it is extremely important to make sure the primary contractor is fully responsible for the finished product. When quality problems develop, the primary supplier will often blame the subcontractor for poor material or workmanship. Of course, the subcontractor will claim that good product was shipped and the fault lies with the primary source. The buyer is faced with trying to resolve the dispute, and it is sometimes difficult to determine where the fault lies. It is therefore important to pinpoint the responsibility with the primary source regardless of who caused the problem. Make the primary source fully responsible.

To avoid disputes between suppliers, buyers often refuse to allow suppliers to subcontract any of the work. However, be aware that even if you do the buying yourself, you may be faced with a similar problem. For example, let's say you buy castings from one source and buy machining from another. You have the completed raw castings sent to the machining source. The machining company claims the castings are too hard or too soft, and that is why the order is being delayed or that is why the parts are defective. The caster claims that good material was shipped to the supplier. You then must figure out who is to blame and take whatever action you feel is appropriate.

One way to minimize these problems is to make sure goods are carefully inspected before sending them to another supplier. If necessary, have castings X-rayed for porosity or otherwise tested to make certain they meet specifications. Make sure you thoroughly investigate suppliers before using them for the first time. Above all, make sure you use the proper source for the proper job. If you need close tolerances or aircraft quality, you may have to pay a little more. If you don't need that level of quality, you are wasting your money by using that type of source.

Terry L. Drews is Senior Buyer for Bellofram Corporation, in Newell, WV.[1] He says that "Tooling is everything when it comes to castings. Metal patterns for sand casting, good quality molds for lost wax (investment cast-ings), or well-designed die cast dies and trim tools are the only way to get good castings." He further states that the buyer should "investigate how a vendor designs, manufactures, and refurbishes tooling before even thinking about doing business with a supplier."

Obtaining Prices and Costs

You can estimate the cost of casting material by knowing the cost of the type of metal that is required and the weight of the rough casting. But you still need to add the cost of the supplier's labor, overhead, and profit require-ment. Obtaining competitive bids and negotiating with the supplier is the best way to zero in on a reasonable price. The buyer should send an engi-neering drawing that shows the shape, dimensions, and type of material required along with the request for bid. A raw casting drawing will have dif-ferent dimensions than a finished machined part. The finished part drawing may be sent in addition to the casting drawing or instead of the casting drawing. The foundry will then calculate how much extra material must be included on the casting to allow for machining or finishing. Most foundries will make drawings or the patterns from a sample part if drawings are not furnished by the customer.

Major variables affecting price include the cost of the type of metal to be used, the amount of the material expressed in pounds or fractions of pounds, the size of the run, and the configuration of the casting. Castings with many holes and requiring cores are more difficult to make than those that are simpler in design.

If you are going to order the castings on a repetitive basis, then you should try to negotiate a firm price plus changes due to economics. If the cost of raw material rises or declines, you would then receive a revised price corresponding to the actual amount of the change. It is smart to limit changes to a certain minimum amount and only to take place at a given time interval. Without doing so, records will need to be constantly changed during a rapidly fluctuating market. In addition, if the cost change affects your products for resale, your selling price would either have to be con-stantly changed as well, or your profits would be affected. Many businesses find it difficult to change prices often.

Pattern prices and other tooling costs such as die cast molds should always be quoted separately and agreed upon before awarding orders to produce the castings even if the tooling is produced in-house by the casting supplier. The buyer should make it clear that the tooling is being purchased and becomes his company's property to remove from the supplier's facilities whenever desired (see Chapter 11 on purchase and control of tooling). Some tooling involves a substantial investment, but it is sometimes possible to get the supplier to help finance the purchase by amortizing the cost over a given period of time, and including it in the price of a given number of pieces of the end product. It is common to require the supplier to maintain the tooling at his expense as long as castings are being purchased from the organization.

It is also wise to negotiate separate pricing for various finishing processes that will be done by the casting company. It then becomes easier to compare costs elsewhere for the raw castings or for machining or any other operation.

Buyers report that prices have been stable for the past half dozen years, although not everyone pays the same and tooling costs vary widely. Terry Drews says that wax molds cost between $3000 and $10,000 depending on the number of cavities. In most cases, die casting dies and trim tools can cost from $5000 to $100,000. The tools can wear out after 250,000 to 350,000 shots (casts). They must be well designed and refurbishable. Cores and ejector pins will need frequent checks for dimensions and performance.

There are foundries in most geographic areas, so if you can find a source that meets your requirements in other respects, you can reduce freight cost by choosing a source that is nearby. On the other hand, there are many low cost sources that produce castings in the Far East or elsewhere. Not too many years ago, significant cost reductions could be obtained by buying from the Pacific Rim countries. Prices now are not as favorable as they were, but savings are still possible. Locations with casting sources include South Korea, Hong Kong, China, and Taiwan. Terms also vary. Some agreements are F.O.B. the seller's plant, some are C.I.F. port of entry.

Before choosing a foreign source, make sure it can meet your quality and delivery requirements. Extra care must be taken when using a foreign source. If for no other reason, longer lead times usually are necessary because of transit time and possible holdups in customs. Reductions in the piece price must be compared to the added cost of insurance, freight, duties, payment terms, and risk of doing business in a foreign country.

Terms Used in the Casting Industry

Cope and Drag: The cope is the top half of a mold, flask (a wooden or metal container for the mold), or pattern. The drag is the bottom half.

Core: An insert into a mold to produce a hole or cavity in the finished product. Cores may be made from "green sand," metal, plastic, or ceramic material.

Expendable Mold Castings: Castings produced from sand molds or other molds wherein the mold is destroyed after the metal is formed.

Flask: The container for the mold and material that makes the mold.

Full Mold Casting: A process that uses a pattern made of expanded polystyrene that is placed in the mold and is vaporized when the molten metal is poured.

Gate: Openings in the mold to control the flow of metal.

Green Sand Castings: Castings produced from natural sand containing moisture and clay holding a mold together. They are the most common type of metal casting and represent approximately 80% of annual production.

Risers: Openings or spaces in the mold that permit molten metal to fill the mold cavity as the metal cools and shrinks and thus maintain the proper size and configuration of the part.

Runner: The channel or down gate that connects the sprue with the casting and that allows the metal to fill the mold.

Shell Mold Casting: An easily automated process that produces expendable shells from metal patterns. The shells produce parts with close tolerances and good surface finish.

Sprue: An opening in the mold that allows molten metal to enter the mold cavity.

Suppliers of Castings

Acme Die Casting Corporation
5626 21st Street

Racine, WI 53406
(414) 554-8887 FAX (414) 554-9503

Acme Die Casting produces aluminum and zinc die castings in two plants with a total of 170,000 square feet. Equipment includes 19 aluminum casting machines ranging in size from 400-ton to 1200-ton, 3 zinc casting machines ranging in size from 400 to 550 tons, 25 trim presses, and 6 furnaces.

Advance Pressure Castings Corporation

276 Hwy. 53, P.O. Box #38
Denville, NJ 07834
(201) 627-6600 FAX (201) 627-0318

Advance Pressure Castings was established in 1932. It produces zinc and aluminum die castings. Equipment includes sixteen 200- to 800-ton locking pressure die casting machines. Casting, machining, finishing, and assembling operations take place in a 65,000 square foot plant. Annual sales are $4.5 million, and the company has 75 employees.

Al Cu Met, Inc.

96 Harvey Road, P.O. Box 1140
Londonderry, NH 03053
(603) 432-6220 FAX (603) 434-7880

Al Cu Met started in 1975. It produces precision nonferrous investment castings in its 30,000 square foot facility. Annual sales are $6 million and there are 100 employees.

Amcast Precision

1100 Jersey Blvd.
Rancho Cucamonga, CA 91730
(909) 987-4721

Amcast produces ferrous and nonferrous castings and vacuum investment castings. It has operations in California and Miami, FL. The company began operations in 1972.

American Cast Iron Pipe Company

American Centrifugal Division
2930 North 16th Street, P.O. Box 2727
Birmingham, AL 35202
(205) 830-8000 FAX (205) 803-3001

American Cast Iron Pipe Company began operations in 1905. It manufactures centrifugally cast steel, iron, and alloy tubes. Facilities cover 2000 acres and the company employees 3100 people.

American Industrial Casting, Inc.
Taylor Precision Casting Division
940 Wellington Avenue
Cranston, RI 02910
(401) 467-4050 FAX (401) 461-4960

American Industrial Casting was established in 1982. It produces nonferrous investment castings in a 16,000 square foot foundry. The company specializes in the manufacture of intricately detailed, tightly dimensioned, thin-walled solid mold nonferrous and shell mold ferrous investment castings. Quantities produced range from prototype to 360 pieces per cavity per hour. Sizes range from subminiature to 3"W X 3"D X 6"H. Alloys of aluminum, bronze, brass, copper, and beryllium copper are produced. Annual sales are reported at $3 million and the company has 44 employees.

Bremen Castings, Inc.
500 N. Baltimore Street
Bremen, IN 46506
(219) 546-2411 FAX (219) 546-5016

Bremen was established in 1939. It produces gray and ductile iron castings from 1/2 to 100 pounds. Machining and painting are available in-house. The company employs 150 people.

BTR Precision Die Casting, Inc.
M & FC Division
Hwy. 68 West, P.O. Box 440
Russellville, KY 42276
(502) 726-0218 FAX (502) 726-6468

BTR was started in 1956. It specializes in thin wall, pressure tight, aluminum die castings ranging in size from 0.06" to 0.25" in wall thickness. Equipment includes 30 machines ranging in size from 600-ton to 1200-ton locking pressure. Annual sales are reported as $50 million and the company has 400 employees.

Clarksville Foundry, Inc.
1140 Red River Street, P.O. Box 786

Clarksville, TN 37041-0786

(615) 647-1538 (615) 645-7207

Clarksville was started in 1847. It produces gray, ductile, and alloy iron as well as stainless steel castings in short to medium runs. It specializes in weights up to 1000 pounds and intricate and cored castings, and pressure container parts. Annual sales are over $2 million. The company employs 40 people.

Connecticut Investment Casting Corporation

75 Stillman Avenue

Pawcatuck, CT 06379

(203) 599-5791 FAX (203) 599-8897

Connecticut Investment Casting was started in 1954. It produces ferrous and nonferrous castings and all air melt alloys. Annual sales are reported at $4 million. The company employs over 45 people.

Joyner's Die Casting and Plating

7801 Xylon Avenue North

Brooklyn Park, MN 55445

(612) 425-1640 FAX (612) 425-2104

Joyner's was established in 1943. It produces zinc die castings from 1/2 ounce to 10 pounds and has complete metal finishing, plating, and painting facilities. It makes nameplates and a standard line of Braille elevator plates and signage. The company employs 75 people.

Engineered Castings, Inc.

1025 S.E. 5th Street

Hialeah, FL 33010

(305) 887-9826 FAX (305) 888-6246

Engineered Castings was established in 1957. It produces aluminum and bronze castings for customers in the medical, aerospace, electronics, marine, aircraft, and OEM industries. It has the capability of producing castings from 1 ounce to 1/4 ton and from 1 piece to 100,000 pieces. The company certifies castings to meet military or special specifications.

HBA Cast Products Company, Inc.

262 Liberty Street

Springfield, MA 01101

(413) 736-1800 FAX (413) 732-1120

HBA began business in 1903. It produces aluminum and zinc alloy using permanent mold, sand, and die castings methods. The company's headquarters and main plant are in Springfield, MA, and a second plant is in Bristol, VA.

Jahn Foundry Corporation
115 Stevens Street
Springfield, MA 01104
(413) 781-3220

The founder of Jahn Foundry Corporation started in the pattern business in 1941 and began a casting foundry in 1944. Since that time, the Jahn Foundry has expanded and developed into a major source for gray iron castings. Operations are in a 140,000 square foot building.

Heick Die Casting Corporation
6550 W. Diversey Avenue
Chicago, IL 60635
(312) 637-1100 FAX (312) 637-1101

Established in 1932, Heick is in a 125,000 square foot facility. It specializes in producing die castings of 390 grade alloy (18% silicon) and pressure-tight applications.

Manger Die Casting Co., Inc.
251 Roosevelt Drive
P.O. Box 322
Derby, CT 06418
(203) 735-7881 FAX (203) 735-4543

Manger began operations in 1956. It produces zinc die castings up to 3 pounds in size. Annual sales are reported at $2 million and the company employs 25 people.

Pittsburgh Die & Casting Company
7503 Ardmore Street
Pittsburgh, PA 15218
(412) 271-5422 or (800) 821-9423 FAX (412) 271-8532

Pittsburgh Die & Casting was established in 1918. It produces custom aluminum and zinc die castings. Facilities include 24,000 square feet of production space and 9200 square feet of storage space. Annual sales are reported at $2 million, and the company employs 30 people.

Prima Die Casting, Inc.
5300 115th Avenue North
Clearwater, FL 34620-4823
(813) 572-7040 FAX (813) 573-0213

Prima was founded in 1965. It produces zinc and aluminum die castings. Reported employment is 85 people.

Quad City Die Casting Company
3800 River Drive
Moline, IL 61265
(309) 762-7346

Quad City Die Casting produces aluminum, magnesium, and zinc die castings. It machines them and finishes them to meet the customer's requirements. Equipment includes 14 die casting machines, 18 trim presses, and numerous lathes, boring machines, and milling machines. The company employs over 150 people.

St. Clair Die Casting
P.O. Box 280
St. Clair, MO 63077
(314) 629-2550 FAX (314) 624-0594

St. Clair Die Casting was started in 1967. It produces custom zinc and aluminum die castings. Annual sales are reported at $20 million and the company has 225 employees.

Thunder Bay Manufacturing Corporation
666 McKinley Avenue
Alpena, MI 49707
(517) 354-3181 FAX (517) 356-1729

Thunder Bay was founded in 1919 and produces gray iron, ductile iron, and alloy castings. Customer drawings or actual parts are used to make patterns of wood or polystyrene in the in-house pattern shop. Small castings to as large as 40 tons are produced for the automotive, stamping, crushing, and grinding, and machine tool industries. There are 100 employees.

Trident Alloys, Inc.
181 Abbe Avenue
Springfield, MA 01107
(413) 737-1477 FAX (413) 737-7924

Trident Alloys, a stainless steel specialty casting company, was established in 1979. It uses a wide range of alloys to make castings in sizes ranging from 1 pound to 2500 pounds. Casting equipment including induction furnaces, heat-treating furnaces, a spectrometer, and a pattern shop are housed in a 22,500 square foot facility. Annual sales are $1.8 million and there are 20 employees.

Vermont American Corporation
Auburn Division
155 Alabama Street
Auburn, AL 36830
(205) 821-7500 FAX (205) 826-3354

Vermont American was started in 1979. The parent company is Emerson Electric Co. The Auburn Division of Vermont American produces investment castings.

West Point Foundry and Machine Co.
301 West Tenth Street, P.O. Box 151
West Point, GA 31833-0151
(706) 643-2127 FAX (706) 643-2100

West Point Foundry and Machine began operations in 1868. It produces gray and ductile iron castings at a melt rate of 5300 pounds per hour. Class 20 to 40 gray iron castings are produced from 1/4 pound to 2500 pounds; ductile iron 65-45-12 castings are produced from 1/4 pound to 1000 pounds. The company also manufactures machinery for the textile industry and builds special machinery to order. The foundry operation covers 25,000 square feet and has 45 employees. Total manufacturing facilities cover 172,000 square feet and employ 300 people.

Associations

American Foundrymen's Society, Inc.
505 State Street
Des Plaines, IL 60016-8399
(708) 824-0181 FAX (708) 824-7848

Diecasting Development Council
6401 Pontiac Drive
La Grange, IL 60525-4394
(708) 246-8840

Non-Ferrous Founders' Society
455 State Street, Suite 100
Des Plaines, IL 60016
(708) 299-0950 FAX (708) 299-3598

North American Die Casting Association
9701 W. Higgins Road, Suite 880
Rosemont, IL 60018-4921
(708) 292-3600 FAX (708) 292-3620

Magazines

Foundry Management & Technology
Penton Publishing Inc.
1100 Superior Avenue
Cleveland, OH 44114-2543
(216) 696-7000 FAX (216) 696-7658

Modern Casting
American Foundrymen's Society (see address, above)

Purchasing
Metals Sourcing Guide 1994
Cahner Publishing Company
275 Washing Street
Newton, MA 02158
(612) 964-3030

Footnotes

[1] Bellofram is a manufacturer of standard and custom-made precision pneumatic control instruments such as air regulators, air relays, transducers, valve positioners, gauge protectors, vane actuators, diaphragm pumps, and other products.

CHAPTER 10

Buying Resin, Plastics, and Ceramics

Thus far we have talked about metals and metal fabrications. Metal substances are classified by the chemist as inorganic material. Nonmetallic material can either be organic or inorganic. Organic material contains elements such as carbon, oxygen, and hydrogen which are all nonmetals. Organic material may be from living things or things that were once alive. Wood is an organic material. Some plastics come from organic material.

About Plastics

The word plastic has more than one meaning. Engineers and scientists talk about the plastic deformation of metals. In laymen's terms that means the ability of the material to have its shape changed without destroying its essential properties. But the layman normally refers to other material when the word plastic is used. It is a material that is made from organic or synthetic substances. Most people think of plastic as a material that is easily bent, although that is not really a necessary part of the definition of what we refer to as plastic. For example, melamine, which is commonly used for such products as kitchen tools, is very hard and fragile. It doesn't bend and will break when dropped.

The molecular structure of plastic materials is very complex and there are thousands of varieties of plastics. However, those varieties can be divided into a few major categories.

Types of Plastic

Plastic materials include various petroleum-derived monomeric and polymeric substances. "Production of plastics follows a well-defined sequence: three primary materials (petroleum, natural gas, and coal) are broken down by refining and fractionation processes into various light-to-heavy petrochemical feedstocks. These materials, also known as light, middle, and heavy oils, are then reacted with others to make more complex intermediates. These can be further reacted with accelerating agents to yield low molecular weight monomers and the heavier, more complex polymers."[1]

Thermoplastics are normally made in large quantities. Typical general-purpose materials are the simpler monomers, such as the polyethylenes, polystyrenes, and polyvinyls. Specialty plastic materials are developed to meet extreme environmental conditions. Such materials involve significant up-front research and development costs. These materials are often produced on a customized basis to address the needs of particular end users. Examples of specialty resins are the cellulosics, the polycarbonates, and the polyetherketones.

Classification of a material is frequently based on how it will be used. Thermoplastics can be reheated and remolded many times, whereas thermosets can be heated and molded to the desired shape only once.

An estimated 66.6 billion pounds of plastic materials were produced in the United States in 1992. The U.S. Department of Commerce/International Trade Administration had forecasted that shipments of plastic and synthetic rubber materials would grow to 5 to 6 percent in 1994; but those numbers will decrease somewhat in the future except for new applications that may develop.

The buyer of plastics may purchase material either as a chemical needing further processing, as a raw material used to make end products, or as an end product ready for final use or resale. The chemicals needed to make plastic material are produced by large chemical companies such as Amoco Chemical Company, E. I. DuPont De Nemours & Co., Mobay Corp., and Rohm and Haas, to mention a few. The chemicals are often products or byproducts of the petrochemical industry, and their price is a function of the price of oil. Therefore, buyers of large quantities of plastic are well advised to pay close attention to the price and supply of oil. Examples of the chemicals used to make plastic material include the following.

Acrylonitrile: A compound with the formula CH_2CHCN. A component of ABS resin providing resistance to chemical attack and heat and adding strength. Present production is estimated at about 1.4 million tons annually.

Butadiene: Used in the production of ABS, nylon, latex paints, and synthetic rubber, and having the formula C_4H_6. One of the components of ABS resin. It provides strength at various temperatures. Annual production is estimated at about 1.6 million tons.

Styrene: Used to make ABS, polystyrene plastics, and rubber. It has the formula $CH_3CH:CH_2$, and is used as component of ABS resin promoting gloss, facilitating processablity, and improving rigidity. Production is about 4.5 million tons annually.

The chemicals make a product that comes out as a powder, or as flakes, or as pellets. The fabricator uses one of these materials to make an end product. The material is first heated. Pressure is then applied to force the soft material into the desired shape for the end product. There are several types of fabricating processes, including injection molding, blow molding, transfer molding, compression molding, extrusion molding, thermoform molding, and rotational molding. Except for the largest, suppliers usually specialize in one type of process. This is probably because the capital equipment is expensive and requires a considerable amount of space. Each piece of equipment requires special knowledge to obtain the best end product.

Injection Molding

Injection molders may have from one or two machines up to hundreds of machines. Depending on the size of the machines and the number of pieces produced by one cycle (shot), they can produce items that weigh only a small fraction of an ounce up to 50 pounds. The machines may be hand fed with the raw material, or automatically fed from elaborate pipes that carry material from silos outside of the building and hundreds of feet away.

There are suppliers in Hong Kong and Taiwan that produce finished products from one or two machines in shops no bigger than a few hundred square feet and with dirt floors. The raw material is stacked to the ceiling and hand dumped into the machines as needed.

There are suppliers with hundreds of machines that use fully automated material-handling equipment that load the raw material on a continual basis and automatically unload the finished product into large bins. These operations can run around the clock with little or no human intervention. One or two workers can handle all of the machines.

Each machine cycles through the following process. The raw material, such as pellets, is dumped into a hopper and fed into a heating chamber to soften it. Other material, such as colorants, may also be fed into the hopper or mixed with the raw material. The softened material is forced into cold dies to obtain the desired shape. The dies separate, the part is ejected, and the dies then close again to accept more material. The dies may be made by the same supplier that produces the finished items, or they may be made by shops that specialize in making dies. The dies are made from metal blocks that have been cut with shapes corresponding to the item to be manufactured. The type of die material used depends on the length of run or volume of goods required as well as the type of plastic to be used. The finish on the die affects the finish on the end product. Dies may be made so that they will be used in a frame. Each die insert contains the shape of the part needed. Thus you may obtain one, two, four, eight, or more parts from one cycle of the injection molding machine, depending on how many inserts are used. Of course, each insert must be machined; so the more inserts you have, the higher the cost of the tool.

By using inserts, you can produce different parts from one cycle of the machine. Thus your cost can be a fraction of the cost of using a machine for one part only. The difficulty with this method is that you must carefully plan the quantities of each item so that you don't obtain too much of one item and not enough of another. With proper planning, the problem can be minimized because you can block off areas of the die by using blank inserts. Alternatively, you can use more space for the same item. For example, if you have room for eight inserts, you might use four inserts for one item, two for another item, and one each for two other items.

When the parts are ejected from the machine, they are connected by flash or thin material that overflows from the die cavity. This flash is easy to remove to separate each item. The removed flash is scrap, but this scrap plus other used plastic is often recyclable with certain types of plastic. In fact, there are special suppliers who sell reprocessed scrap, and such pellets are less expensive than new material.

Blow Molding

When you want a hollow plastic item produced, such as a bottle or other container, blow molding may be the best way of obtaining what you need

Figure 10-1. Blow molded plastic items. (Courtesy of Crocker Limited.)

at the lowest cost. The process involves heating appropriate resin for your purposes in the hopper of a machine designed to produce blow molded parts. The softened material is formed into a hollow tube. The thickness of the wall of the tube determines the thickness of the finished item. Air under pressure is injected into the tube and forces the sides to expand to fit a set of dies. The dies separate and the hardened part is ejected from the machine. At this stage, the part may be already finished except for removal of any flash. Blow molding machines come in various sizes and designs, but basically perform similar operations.

Transfer Molding

In the transfer molding process, a product is made by measuring a calculated quantity of thermoset plastic. Extra material is used to assure complete filling of the mold. The measured raw material may be granular or preformed. It is heated in a chamber of the transfer mold machine, and the softened material is forced into a mold through openings called sprues and runners designed into the mold for that purpose. Then pressure is applied until the plastic cures. The mold is then opened and the item removed. If the desired product requires hollow spaces, reusable cores may be inserted into the mold. This extra material, called cull, is attached to the finished part by runners when it is removed from the mold with the good part. Both the runners and the cull are removed from the finished parts.

Compression Molding

In the compression molding process, the raw material is placed in an open mold. The mold is then closed and pressure and heat are applied to form the shape of the part. The mold is then opened and the part removed.

Extrusion Molding

Plastic as well as metal items are produced by the extrusion process. A die is used with an opening designed to produce the shape desired. The heated raw material is forced through the die opening to produce the product.

Thermoform Molding

In the thermoform molding process, a sheet or film of thermoplastic is heated and pressed against a mold by air, a vacuum, or mechanically to obtain the desired shape that may be up to 300 square feet in size.

Rotational Molding

The rotational molding process is also referred to as the rotational casting process. It is used to make hollow plastic articles primarily from thermoplastics. Either a solid or liquid raw material is placed in the mold. The mold is heated and then cooled while rotating. Large items can be produced, and the process involves low tooling and equipment cost.

It is easy to locate a supplier to make a plastic part. There are hundreds to choose from and it is a very competitive market. However, it is not easy for the buyer to find the very best supplier to make what a company needs. There are many factors and variables to be considered. Of course, price should always be a major consideration even though some companies may say price is no object. Other factors are quality, quantity needed, consistency, stability, delivery on schedule, and long-term costs. The buyer must determine the priorities before selecting a source.

Take, for example, the buyer with a major Fortune 500 company that placed orders for small plastic parts used in computers. The price was good and the quality was satisfactory, but the supplier was consistently behind schedule. As time passed, the behind-schedule condition became worse and worse. Promises were made to ship 100,000 by Friday, but only 75,000 were shipped. The supplier made a new promise on Monday to make up the difference in the new week, but instead fell further behind. An on-site review determined that the machines could not possibly produce the needed quantities even though they worked twenty-four hours a day, seven days a week. Obviously either the source was originally the wrong choice or the forecast of needs were incorrectly made.

About Ceramics

If you buy a ceramic product, you may have a different impression of what ceramics are than other buyers do. That is because there are many types of ceramics, and they are used for many different purposes. Any one buyer may only be familiar with one or several ceramic products.

Dictionaries give an inadequate definition of ceramics. Encyclopedias explain more but tend to stress particular types of ceramic products or applications; for example, there may be a lengthy discussion of the design of pottery. Formerly ceramics referred to pottery making, but now the term includes the technology of manufacturing of products out of certain compounds of metallic and nonmetallic elements. Clay, cement, plaster, gypsum, abrasives, glass, porcelain enamel, and refractories are all considered ceramics. They have the common characteristics of being hard, brittle, and nonconductors of electricity. They have a very high melting point which is used to advantage in lining ovens and furnaces and covering the nose cone of reentry vehicles from outerspace. They resist corrosion and are therefore often used for storage containers for highly reactive chemicals such as strong acids.

Ceramic raw materials are often found in the natural state, but some are man made and some of those are patented. The word ceramic is derived from the Greek, keramos, meaning "a potter" or "a pottery." The Greek word is related to a Sanskrit root meaning "to burn." The combination of these meanings describe the ceramic product as burned earth. Fired clay used to make products is the oldest material used by man. The use of pottery made of clay goes back to the Stone Age. Cement, another type of

Figure 10-2a. Ceramic substrate lapping and polishing process. (Courtesy of Coors Ceramics Company.)

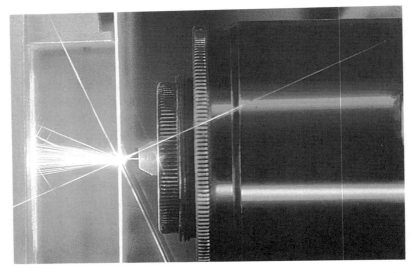

Figure 10-2b. CO_2 laser machining a ceramic substrate. (Courtesy Coors Ceramics Company.)

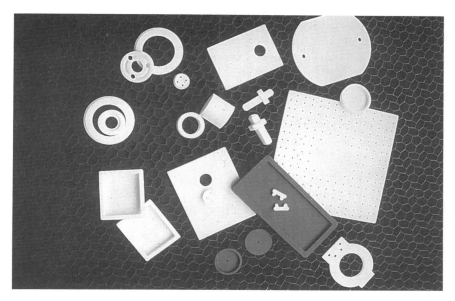

Figure 10-2c. Dry-pressed microceramic parts. (Courtesy Coors Ceramics Company.)

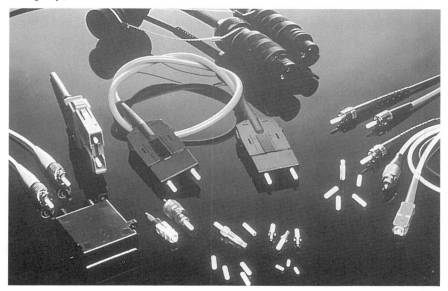

Figure 10-2d. Zirconia ferrules and examples of fiber-optic connectors in which they are used. (Courtesy Coors Ceramics Company.)

ceramic, was used for construction by the ancient Romans; they combined volcanic ash, lime, clay, and water.

But don't be misled, the use of ceramics today is in highly sophisticated products for medical equipment, electronic devices, aerospace, automotive, and other high-tech industries, as well as in the construction trades and consumer market.

Depending on various definitions used, ceramics can apply to traditional products, or can refer to the manufacturing technology required to make ceramic products, or it can refer to various engineering materials used in manufacturing.

Manufacturing Methods

Almost all ceramic products are produced from various types of natural clay found in the earth. The clay is usually refined to various degrees, and the chemical composition altered by additions of certain compounds to satisfy the requirements of the end product. Silica sand, quartz rock, flint pebbles, or other material called fillers are often added to increase the strength of the final product. Fluxes are added to promote fusion of the material. Potassium oxide or sodium oxide are commonly added fluxes. The raw material is then shaped and formed in molds. Different methods are used for softer or stiffer raw material. For soft raw material, small quantities may be formed by hand or using a wheel. For high production forming of clay material that has a highly plastic rheology, techniques known as jiggering, jolleying, and ram pressing are used. Forming of stiffer material is accomplished by several different extrusion methods. Uniaxial pressing is another method used. It compresses a powder raw material in a die. Isostatic pressing applies equal pressure to all surfaces of a formed item that has been placed in a sealed liquid. Modern ceramic manufacturing uses computer-controlled equipment to provide a high-quality consistent product.

After forming, the product is fired or baked. The temperature depends on the type of clay and its components as well as the desired use of the product. Finished products may be either glazed or not glazed. The glaze may have either a sheen or dull finish. The glaze is applied to the formed product as a suspension of various ingredients in water. Firing of the product may be accomplished in one step after the glaze is applied, or the product may be fired twice — once before the glaze and once after the glaze.

The Ceramic Industry

In 1992, *Ceramic Industry* magazine conducted a survey of 443 major ceramic producers worldwide. They reported a total of $82 billion in sales broken down in the following percent of sales and dollar sales in millions by product class.

Glass	54%	$44,152.30
Advanced ceramics	19%	$15,342.00
Whiteware	10%	$ 8,223.20
Porcelain enamel	9%	$ 7,670.00
Refractories	7%	$ 5,856.90
Structural clay	1%	$ 1,011.00

Only ten of the top companies accounted for 51% of the total sales. Leading the list of the four U.S. companies in the top ten was General Electric in fourth place, followed by Owens-Illinois in sixth place, Whirlpool in ninth place, and PPG in tenth.

The magazine reported that more than 132 firms participated in the advanced ceramic market segment. The leading company was Philips Electronics N.V. based in the Netherlands. In the top ten of this segment there were six Japanese companies, namely, Kyocera, Murats Mfg. Co. Ltd., Sumitomo Electric Industries, Ltd., NGK Insulators Ltd., Asahi, and Sony Corp. Ltd. Corning was the only U.S. company in the top five.

As is the case with certain metals, you may feel locked in to buy a certain product only produced by one source because an engineer or designer specified that brand of material. Keep in mind that there may be a generic equivalent or another material with only a slightly different formula that will do the job. It is not unusual to find a standard material that does a better job and at a significantly lower cost.

Ceramic clay materials of various types are used to make china, earthenware, porcelain, and stoneware. The clay used to make china contains quartz and feldspar. This translucent clay is fired at high temperatures to produce dinnerware and other products. Earthenware requires a clay material called kaolin to make a type of dinnerware and drain tile. It is produced at a lower temperature than that required by china. Porcelain is produced at very high temperatures for products requiring a hard corrosive resistant finish. Stoneware is produced with high temperatures and is used for ovenware products.

Glass is another ceramic material with many varieties and many applications. All of these products are subjects unto themselves, but that is especially the case with glass.

A very important ceramic application is in the production of refractories. They are used to line furnaces and ovens especially in the iron and steel industry which accounts for 63% of refractory consumption in the United States.

Some Technical Terms Used in the Ceramic Industry

Argillaceous: Like or containing clay.

Fillers: Material added to clay to add strength to the final product.

Fluxes: A substance added to a material to help it fuse better.

Jiggering: Involves the placement of an extruded slug of raw material on a revolving plaster form. A tool cuts away material as the slug revolves.

Jolleying: Similar to jiggering except for the use of the cutting tool. The tool may be heated to form a steam cushion to prevent sticking to the slug.

Rheology: The study of the deformation and flow of matter.

Slip Casting: A process whereby excess liquid material is poured away before it hardens.

Sample Suppliers of Plastics and Ceramics

B & D Molded Products, Inc.
Oliver Terrace, P.O. Box 306
Shelton, CT 06484
(203) 929-1441, FAX (203) 929-6471

B & D started in 1959. It has 75 employees and $7 million in sales volume. The company has 100,000 square feet of manufacturing space producing blow molded balls, wheels, cases, and toys. B & D specializes in polyethylene products.

Coors Ceramics Company
Electronic Products Group
17750 W. 32nd Avenue
Golden, CO 80401
(303) 277-4802

It has been more than 30 years since Coors developed a highly reliable bond between ceramic and metal. Today, its custom-made metallized parts can be found in everything from computers to automobiles. Coors Ceramics Company's Electronic Products Group manufactures advanced technical ceramics for the microelectronics industry. Primary product lines include ceramic substrates for microelectronic circuitry, laser-machined ceramic substrates, dry pressed ceramics, metallized ceramics, and glass-to-metal seals. It is the largest domestic supplier for electronic ceramic components worldwide.

Crocker Limited
1510 N. Main Street
Three Rivers, MI 49093
(616) 279-5275, FAX (616) 279-9716

Crocker started in 1973. It has 160 employees and 100,000 square feet of manufacturing facilities. Two plants, one in Three Rivers, MI, and one in Centreville, MI. Twenty molding machines range in size from 1-pound to 25-pound shot capability. The company specializes in quality blow molding of hollow plastic parts, and it serves the housewares, hardware, construction, small engine, seating and furniture, packaging, appliance, material handling, automotive, recreational, toy, lawn and garden, marine, military, and medical industries.

Eckert Manufacturing Company
3820 Nicholson Road, P.O. Box 828
Fowlerville, MI 48836
(517) 521-4905, FAX (517) 521-4172

Eckert started in 1966. It produces injection molded items and has in-house tooling facilities.

Ipsen Ceramics
Division of Abar Ipsen Industries
325 John Street, P.O. Box 420
Pecatonica, IL 61063
(815) 239-2385 FAX (815) 239-2387

Ipsen began operations in 1954. The company produces a variety of ceramic products including coarse grained, porous compositions for brick, trays, piers, and mufflers; fine grained products for tubes and rollers; round and flat bottom crucibles; and refractories.

Kyocera America, Inc.
Microelectronics Division
8611 Balboa Avenue
San Diego, CA 92123-1580
(619) 576-2600 FAX (619) 569-9412

Kyocera began business in 1969. It produces ceramic IC packaging. The company employs 800 people.

Lanxide Corporation
1300 Marrows Road, P.O. Box 6077
Newark, DE 19714-6077
(302) 456-6200 FAX (302) 454-1712
Telex 905019 LANXIDE

Lanxide Corporation was founded in Newark, DE, in 1983 to develop and commercialize a new approach to the manufacture of reinforced metals and ceramics. Lanxide™ composites possess combinations of strength, toughness, hardness, damage tolerance, shape and size versatility, stiffness, chemical stability, and temperature tolerance. The company has over 3200 issued or pending patents. Facilities include 320,000 square feet of laboratory, manufacturing, and office space. Lanxide has joint ventures with E. I. du Pont de Nemours and Company, Kanematsu Corporation, and other partners. The company has more than $300 million in resources and employs 375 people.

Mindrum Precision, Inc.
10,000 4th Street
Rancho Cucamonga, CA 91730
(909) 989-1728 FAX (909) 987-3709

Mindrum Precision was started in 1956. It produces custom precision glass, quartz, and ceramic components and assemblies such as dampers, flow cells, and hermetic windows. Annual sales are reported at $3 million and the company has 50 employees.

Patron Plastics, Inc.
2776 Albrecht Avenue
Akron, OH 44312
(216) 794-0013 FAX (216) 794-0243

Patron started in 1978. It has 70 employees with sales volume of $4 million. Its 30,000 square foot facility blow molds items ranging in size from 1/4 to 5 pounds.

Plasticraft Manufacturing Company, Inc.
115 Plasticraft Drive
Albertville, AL 35950
(205) 828-4105 FAX (205) 891-1177

Plasticraft started in 1972. It has 75 employees, and sales of $5 million plus. The plant has 120,000 square feet of manufacturing facilities. It produces both injection and blow molded proprietary stock, and custom nylon, ABS, and polyethylene knobs for the medical, scientific, power tool, lawn and garden equipment, photographic equipment, athletic apparatus, home appliances, and automobile industries.

Res-Tech Corporation
28 Marshall Street
Clinton, MA 01510
(508) 368-0146 FAX (508) 365-5958

Res-Tech started in 1976. It has 85 employees, and sales of $6 million. There are two plants with a combined area of 40,000 square feet, including a tool shop and 29 injection molding machines. Its customers are in the medical, computer, computer peripheral, electronic, photographic, and laboratory application industries.

Superior Technical Ceramics Corp.
P.O. Box 1028
St. Albans, VT 05478
(802) 527-7726 FAX (802) 527-1181

Superior Technical Ceramics began operations in 1898. It produces technical ceramics using extrusion, dry pressing, isopressing, injection molding, green forming, and diamond machining manufacturing methods. The primary materials used are alumina, zirconia, steatite, cordierite, mullite, and lava. Customers include those in the heliarc welding, plasma cutting, aerospace, medical, and OEM instrumentation and equipment industries.

Thermal Ceramics

P.O. Box 923
Augusta, GA 30903
(706) 796-4200 FAX (706) 796-4328

Thermal Ceramics began operations in 1928. It produces a wide selection of high-temperature insulating refractories. It produces ceramic fiber products, fire protection products, refractory monolithics, engineered fiber products, firebrick, insulating products, fired refractory shapes, and vermiculite and diatomaceous silica products. It has sales offices in eighteen states and has nine affiliated companies.

Wesgo, Inc.

477 Harbor Blvd.
Belmont, CA 94002
(415) 598-3239 FAX (415) 598-3236

Wesgo was started in 1927. The company produces technical ceramics and braze alloys. The parent company is Morgan Crucible Company. It has manufacturing facilities in Fairfield, NJ, in addition to the plant in Belmont.

Associations

The American Ceramic Society
735 Ceramic Place
Westerville, OH 43081-8720
(614) 793-4810 FAX (614) 899-6109

Magazines and Periodicals

Modern Plastics
Published by McGraw-Hill, Inc.
Editorial Offices

1221 Sixth Avenue
New York, NY 10020
(212) 512-6242 FAX (212) 512-6111
Subscription Inquiries: (609) 426-7070 FAX (609) 426-5905

Plastics World
PTN Publishing Co.
445 Broad Hollow Road, Ste 21
Melville, NY 11747
(516) 845-2700 FAX (516) 845-7109

Ceramic Industry
Business News Publishing Company
775 W. Big Beaver Road, Suite 1000
Troy, MI 48084-4900
Circulation Department: 5900 Harper Road, Suite 109
Solon, OH 44139-1835
(216) 498-9214 FAX (216) 498-9121

Footnotes

[1] U.S. Industrial Outlook 1994, U.S. Department of Commerce/International Trade Administration, January 1994.

CHAPTER **11**

Purchasing and Controlling Tooling and Scrap[1]

There are two additional areas that buyers of production material often handle and are responsible for: 1) the purchase of tooling necessary to make various components; and 2) the disposal of scrap generated when production items are made.

All About Tooling

In many instances, it is necessary to buy dies, jigs, fixtures, artwork, or other reusable items necessary to produce another proprietary product being purchased. In such cases, the buyer often pays for these items, and so they should become the property of the buyer. If further orders are placed for fabricated products with that supplier or with any other supplier, it should not be necessary to buy the tooling again if the tooling is still adequate. It is the responsibility of the buyer to see that a detailed and up-to-date record is made documenting ownership of such goods.

If you buy printing, corrugated boxes, metal stampings, die castings, or any other product made to your unique specifications, custom tooling is required before those items can be produced.[2] Cutting dies are needed for corrugated containers. Plates are needed for printing. Molds and dies are needed for plastic parts and metal stampings. Occasionally the cost of such tooling may be buried or concealed in the piece price, but normally buyers issue separate purchase orders for the tooling, or they at least list it as a separate item on the order. Often a different source is used to make the tooling, although the supplier of the finished product may select that source and place the order. Unless the company buying the finished product has a highly capable engineering department that insists on designing the tools, it is usually best to let the finished goods supplier select the tool maker. This is because the tools need to be compatible with machines and equipment of the finished goods manufacturer. However, the buyer needs to make sure that charges for tooling are controlled, and that the tooling is not designed so as to preclude its use elsewhere. The cost of production tools used to produce custom items may vary from less than $100 to hundreds of thousands of dollars. It is not at all unusual to spend over $100,000 for a mold or die. Sometimes you have a choice whether you want to spend a little or a lot depending on the amount of the finished product you intend to buy over a period of time, and depending on how quickly you want deliveries. Bigger or more durable expensive tooling will produce the items faster or will last longer. Any given supplier may not offer the buyer a choice simply because it does not have the machinery for more than one size or type of tooling. One supplier may only have large or fast equipment that is ideally suited for large quantities. Another supplier may have small or slow machinery. The former type of equipment will most likely take higher cost tooling than the latter. It is up to the buyer to shop for the appropriate source for the long-term quantities and deliveries needed.

If a supplier has both types of equipment, you may get a quotation based on two types of tooling. The piece price of the finished goods may be different depending on which machines are used, and it probably should be so because the supplier's cost will be different. It is not as simple as making the right decision on the piece price alone. You must decide if it is worth it to buy the more expensive tooling. If your consideration is based ultimately on the right cost decision, you must know at what quantity it will be better to buy the higher priced tooling.

Take the following hypothetical example. Suppose a supplier offers to produce widgets for you at 50¢ each and a tooling cost of $500, or at a piece price of 35¢ each but with a tooling cost of $1000. What is your choice? It all depends on the volume you expect to buy. You need to know at what volume it is best to pick the $500 tooling charge, and at what volume the $1000 charge is a more economical choice. Just make a simple equation with the tooling and the associated piece price on one side equal to the alternative choice on the other side. Take the general case:

$$T1 + P1V = T2 + P2V$$

where

$T1$ = the lower tooling cost or $500
$P1$ = piece price or the associated cost of 50¢
V = the volume we want to know
$T2$ = the higher tooling cost or $1000
$P2$ = piece price or the associated cost of 35¢

If you substitute the figures and solve for V, you get an answer of 3333 pieces. In other words, at that volume it would not matter which tooling you buy; the total expenditures for tooling and product would be the same. However, at any lower volume, you would be better off buying the less expensive tooling, whereas at any higher volume you should choose the more costly tooling. This calculation ignores the amount of money and the number of years you plan to buy the product, but for relatively short periods you may find it sufficient. If the supplier insists that piece price is the same regardless of volume, then you should still be concerned with delivery and how long you are going to need the tooling. Make your estimate carefully — either underestimating or overestimating can be costly.

Record Keeping

Purchase orders should include a description of the tooling and a clause indicating that the described tooling becomes the property of the buying company. Wherever possible, the cost or price of the tooling should be obtained separately from the primary product and be stated separately on the purchase order and on the invoice from the supplier. Unless the cost of the tooling is to be amortized over a specified period of time or specified quantity of the primary product, the charge for the tooling should be clearly indicated as a one-time charge. An inventory of all company-owned tooling held by suppliers should be maintained and available to accounting personnel upon request. The record should indicate a description of the tooling and its purpose, the date of purchase, the purchase order number, the supplier's name and address, and the location of the tooling if other than the supplier's office address.

Responsibility for Maintenance

The buyer should clearly establish to the supplier that the tooling must be maintained properly while in the supplier's possession. A record should be kept of any necessary maintenance and be available to the buyer upon request, or routinely sent to the buyer if the buyer so wishes. Maintenance cost is often routinely conducted by suppliers at no cost to the buyer in order to assure continual business. Storage charges for the tooling are usually absorbed by the seller unless no orders have been received from the buyer for an extended period of time. The seller should inform the buyer well before any storage charges are applied. In such cases, the buyer must decide the merits of having the tooling brought in-house or disposing of the tooling if it is no longer needed. Before disposal, both the market value and the book value must be clearly determined so that all appropriate action can be taken.

Responsibility for Insurance

It is the responsibility of the buyer to make sure that the supplier has insurance to cover company-owned tooling in the supplier's possession. If the supplier does not have or is unable or unwilling to obtain insurance for company property, the buyer should determine if his company's insurance covers property held at a supplier. If not, the advisability of obtaining such insurance should be discussed with company management. The cost of such insurance should be compared to the risk involved.

Buyer's Exclusive Use

The buyer should make certain that the supplier understands that the buyer's organization's tooling must not be used to produce goods for any other customer. While this seldom happens, a supplier who does so causes several problems for the owner of the tooling. First, the tooling wears out more quickly. Second, the tooling may be producing items that are going into a competitor's product. The manufacturer may be charging both customers for the tooling, or the competitor may be obtaining the goods at a lower cost because he doesn't have to pay for tooling. A statement prohibiting use of the tooling for any other customer should be included in the purchase agreement or on the purchase order.

This problem can be partially prevented by including logos, certain markings, or design features in the dies or molds so that the finished item would show what tooling was used; but the manufacturer may be able to work around markings by various devices during the manufacturing process.

Using International Sources for Tooling

Substantial cost savings can often be obtained by having tooling made overseas; for example, Portugal has the reputation of producing good molds and dies. Several caveats are called for. It is sometimes necessary to have engineers travel to the foreign country to check the supplier's capability or discuss technical problems with the supplier's engineers. The possibility of this extra cost for traveling should be considered before a sourcing decision is made. The buyer should check to see if any import duties are involved and add those costs as well. Although English is spoken by many business people and many technical people in most foreign countries, it is still difficult to communicate when discussing technical problems. In most cases, especially for small savings, it is probably better to use a foreign source for tooling only when the production product is to be supplied from that country.

Negotiate Amortized Cost

Once in a while, the buyer will run across a supplier who will pay for the tooling and amortize the cost into the piece price. The buyer should keep track of the amount in the piece price that is attributable to tooling and how many pieces of the product are purchased. Usually such agreements stipulate the quantity of parts and how soon that quantity will be scheduled.

It is absolutely essential that the details of the agreement are carefully documented and that the written agreement indicates that the tooling is being purchased and is the property of the buyer.

Control and Disposal of Scrap, Surplus Inventory, and Equipment

Nearly every organization that deals with a tangible product generates scrap of some nature. Even many service companies — and certainly the government — generate enormous amounts of scrap paper through the use of forms. Quite often, the responsibility for the disposal of various types of scrap is assigned to the purchasing function.

While at first glance this may seem odd, especially to those whose primary function is the purchase of goods and services, closer analysis reveals the logic of such delegation. Buyers of the products that produce scrap are probably more familiar with the marketplace than are other employees within the organization. In addition, they can often work with suppliers during the initial purchase of material to establish specifications that will limit the amount of scrap generated.

Suppliers of the new material often may be able to recycle the scrap, and then can provide price or cost incentives for scrap that is returned for reuse. Similar arrangements can often be made for excess inventory. The supplier may be able to take it back, usually at a substantial discount, and then resell it to other customers. Obviously, the better the condition of the material, the more likely the supplier will be to accept it, and the more likely a higher price will be paid.

The best time to negotiate with a supplier about the sale or use of scrap and possible excess inventory is before new material is purchased. This is not always possible, but some suppliers will make an agreement for the repurchase or credit for scrap as a buyer incentive in order to obtain an order for new material. In many cases, they are incurring little risk since there will be little or no scrap generated from the use of the material. And if the material is new, unused inventory, it can be resold at a profit. Keep in mind that excess inventory is not likely to be saleable if it is unique or made to your company's specifications. Standard items are relatively easy to dispose of.

Restocking charges for material returned quickly after purchase will be minimal. Sometimes full credit will be given. The longer you wait, the less likely you will get a good price for returned material.

Most suppliers will not pay for returned merchandise but will give the buyer credit against future orders. However, material can sometimes be sold to companies that are not the normal source of supply. It depends on the type of material, the state of the market for the items in question, and the condition of the material.

The buyer can usually obtain better prices if he or she is able to return goods to the original supplier rather than a scrap dealer. Scrap dealers normally pay a small percentage of the original value. Prices vary widely, again depending on the condition, the marketplace, and the type of material. Markets for some materials are fairly steady, while other materials fluctuate radically. There are times when you can't give certain types of scrap away.

Obtaining the Best Price

Because the condition of the material affects the price you receive, it is important to protect goods and store them properly. Make sure that inventory or even scrap is protected from the elements as much as possible. You may see steel products piled outside and exposed to rain and snow. In time, such material becomes rusted and severely pitted so that its value is sharply reduced. It may still have value as scrap, but chances are that it will not be acceptable for use as originally intended.

Tip: Be alert to the condition of material stored for use at a fabricator or other type of supplier. That supplier may not be as interested in protecting the material as you are. Have it physically checked once in a while to make sure it is stored and handled properly.

Know the Market

In order to get the best price for scrap, you should be familiar with the scrap market. Variables that affect price include time of the year, type of product, condition of the product, where it is physically located, and the demand for the product. Sometimes it is impossible to sell a particular item. At other times, the same item brings in a good price. Following is a partial list of scrap items that have value or have had value at one time or another:

Paper and paper products
    Computer punch cards
    Newsprint
    Corrugated
Plastic
Copper
Steel
Aluminum
Gold — computer boards
Oil
Chemicals

Storage and Preparation

A much better price can be obtained if scrap is separated by product or raw material type. It may pay to disassemble items and then segregate the different types of components. For example, mixing aluminum and steel can destroy the scrap value of both products. Items with coatings may have less value than those without. Some plastics can be recycled, some cannot.

Shop and Negotiate

Selling scrap requires many of the skills and techniques of good buying. You need to obtain bids, check the reputation of the company you are dealing with, and negotiate to obtain the best price. Certain periodicals publish scrap prices for many items. Although the published prices may be for slightly different products, you may be able to get an idea of market conditions and the relative value of your scrap material. Check magazines or periodicals such as the *American Metal Market* or *The Wall Street Journal*.

Offer a long-term agreement to sell your scrap to a certain source in order to get a better price. The amount could be based on what you generate or a fixed amount that you are sure you will have within a certain length of time. You can tie the actual price to an index or to a published market average. You might get an agreement that gives you a price at a certain percentage below that average. Potential customers for scrap, excess inventory, and obsolete material include the following;

Regular suppliers of the new material
Scrap dealers
Competitors
Companies that use secondary material
Auction houses

Limiting Scrap Generation and Excess Inventory

Scrap generation and excess inventory are normally the responsibility of plant management or operation management, but the buyer has partial responsibility and can do much to help with the control. Someone needs to keep records; if this is not done elsewhere, it should be done by the person or department that disposes of the material.

Personnel need to be trained to minimize the generation of scrap, and the disposal of scrap must be controlled to minimize cost.

Keeping Records

A record of the amount of scrap, the type of scrap, and related information helps trace responsibility, determines the cost, and provides information to reduce the amount generated. The date of sale and quantities sold are valuable data needed to properly analyze what is going on and point the way for improvement.

Good inventory records showing the amount ordered, the date ordered, the amount used, and the balance on hand are essential for inventory control. These data, combined with good sales forecasts and up-to-date marketing information, provide the inputs to minimize excess inventory.

Training Employees

The person responsible for the sale of scrap should quickly determine what items need to be segregated in order to maximize the amount realized. This information should be passed along to operating management or conveyed to those generating the scrap so they can handle it properly.

Provide Incentives

Companies have offered prizes and awards to individuals and departments that can reduce or eliminate scrap. For example, when curved windshields were first introduced, a very high percentage cracked as the automobiles were being assembled. Those on the assembly line were offered free dinners at a fancy restaurant if they could complete a certain number of vehicles without breaking a windshield. Breakage dropped sharply as a result.

Control Disposal

There are all sorts of horror stories about abuses related to scrap and inventory control. Some involve carelessness and poor quality control. Some involve cheating. Some are criminal acts that may cost organizations hundreds of thousands to millions of dollars.

When bumpers were made of steel plated with chrome, they were attached to the vehicle with bolts that were similarly plated. Those bumpers and bolts were among the most expensive items in the vehicle. In at least one instance, thousands were left over after that model year and the quantity far exceeded what could be used as service replacement parts. Company management issued orders to have all the excess bumpers cut in half with a torch and each threaded bolt struck with a sledge hammer to ruin the threads. Only after this was done were the items to be sent to the scrap dealers.

This seemingly extreme and costly action was taken to prevent the items from reaching the aftermarket and competing with company sales. Defective and substandard items that may be resold as authentic new product may damage the reputation of an organization producing a quality product.

While it may be routine to have scrap dealers or others sign an agreement not to resell the goods as new goods, it may not be enough. It may be necessary to obliterate company names, logos, insignias, or any other identifying marks. It may be necessary to damage the goods further to prevent normal use.

Internal control is also important. Employees may deliberately generate scrap in collusion with a scrap dealer in order to get a "kickback." There are instances where perfectly good material is tossed into scrap containers. The causes of scrap generation should be carefully investigated. While a certain amount of scrap, excess inventory, or obsolete material is to be expected in the course of business, excessive, unnecessary quantities can be controlled and must be controlled to minimize costs. Sometimes it is a question of being profitable or not.

Types of Controls to Implement

Allowing scrap dealers to have free access to plant floors can be a mistake. They may not always be careful enough in choosing the scrap items to collect, and may accidentally or deliberately collect good material when they pick up the scrap items.

The person responsible for selling scrap should make certain that scrap dealer trucks used in collecting metal turnings are weighed empty and weighed after collecting the scrap from certified controlled public scales and that documentation is provided. It is best to have a company employee or security guard go to the scales to verify that the truck was empty.

Footnotes

[1] A portion of this chapter was taken with permission from the generic policy and procedure manual published by the American Purchasing Society.

[2] A portion of this chapter was taken from an article in *Professional Purchasing*, February 1994.

CHAPTER 12

Source Selection Issues and Resolving Purchasing Problems

Various methods used to locate a source were discussed in Chapter 2, but some important and perhaps subtle considerations in the selection of a source were not given. This chapter will discuss some of the issues that a buyer should think about before deciding on which source to buy from and how to place business.

Large versus Small Suppliers[1]

There are advantages to using large suppliers, and different advantages to using small suppliers. Large suppliers have more funds available for investment in tooling, equipment, and research. Small suppliers have relatively smaller staff functions and lower overhead costs. Large suppliers may be able to buy the products and services they need at lower prices because of volume purchases. Small suppliers may be able to deliver more quickly because of less red tape. Managers and other employees at small companies usually have more authority to make decisions, while those in large organizations may have to go through several levels of the organization in order to get answers. The savvy buyer should be aware of these differences and give them sufficient weight when making a decision about which supplier to use. Sometimes it is far better to use the large supplier. Other times, it is to your advantage to use a capable small supplier.

The differences between large and small companies may not always be apparent. For example, large suppliers may well understand your requests for a detailed breakdown of costs or your requests for the supplier's financial statements. They probably have dealt with those types of requests before and will have no reluctance in giving you the information. In many cases, some information is public anyway because the company is listed on the stock exchange. Small companies, especially private ones, often feel such financial information is confidential and they resist providing it. They may be even more reluctant to give the buyer cost data. They don't understand the win–win negotiating method and may misunderstand the buyer's motives. On the other hand, if the buyer can sell the advantages of sharing information and teach the smaller supplier the ways of big business, the smaller business can pass along its lower costs in the form of substantial savings to the buyer.

Purchasing from Divisions and Subsidiaries of Large Companies

It is easy to buy from a division or subsidiary of a large company without realizing that the entity is affiliated with a larger organization. To assess the merits of buying from a particular supplier, the buyer should ascertain if the potential supplier is independent or affiliated with another company. The degree of independence and amount of centralized support and control should be determined.

The large company can provide financial strength to the division. It can also pull the rug out from under an unprofitable division or subsidiary. The large company can decide to close down a division without much warning to even those who are employed in that division. This can seriously disrupt a source of supply. While most large companies will attempt to satisfy customers for a certain period of time, it is not uncommon for some to all but ignore the customer's problems.

Conversely, if you depend on the large company to enforce good performance by a division or subsidiary, you may be disappointed. The parent company may simply refer complaints from a buyer back to the division for resolution without any pressure being applied to help the buyer.

Domestic versus International

There are two major reasons for buying from an international source. The first and foremost reason — when you have a real choice — is to get a lower cost. Prices are frequently much lower in foreign countries, particularly in the Third World countries and the Pacific Rim countries (with the possible exception of Japan). Not too many years ago, sourcing to Japan could provide a real cost advantage. Since the value of the yen has increased, that is no longer true, in most cases.

The buyer should be careful but not timid about investigating the possibilities in choosing a foreign source. Although you must consider import duties, ocean or air transportation costs, insurance costs, and paper handling costs, the potential for significant savings is great. However, in addition to those obvious cost factors, you must add the risk of fluctuating monetary exchange rates, and the risk of dealing with a supplier thousands of miles away. Although it provides an advantage, the buyer need not travel to the foreign location or speak the foreign language. (Most foreigners know English but not always fluently.) Nor does the buyer need to know how to determine duty rates, routing, or the rules in preparing the import documents. Custom house brokers will do all this for you at a very reasonable rate.

But there are other problems to be considered. There is a longer lead time — it can be *much* longer. There may be risk of changes in government policy to prohibit buying from certain countries, or to impose a higher duty. There may be political or other disturbances in the foreign country that cause delays in shipments. Domestic suppliers may resent buyers who buy from foreign competition and take action to curtail domestic supply, especially during periods of short supply or allocation. This author's experience is that this is more often a subtle or implied threat rather than real.

In spite of all the problems, the smart buyer still checks the advantages against the disadvantages and gives each set its proper weight without exaggeration.

The second reason to buy from a foreign source is because you have no choice — i.e., the product is only made or produced in a foreign country. There are many valuable items produced elsewhere, but unless the buyer keeps an open mind and shops the world, he or she may never know about those products and the advantages they offer to a business. Good buyers are not provincial. They understand that you may have to leave your own backyard to find gold.

How Many Sources to Use

Purchasing professionals who entered the function many years ago will remember the stress placed on having more than one source for the same item, particularly production items. The reason given was to make certain that there would always be enough material if one supplier failed. In recent years, there has been strong advocacy of single sourcing. With single sourcing, the buying company becomes a partner with the supplier. Both companies benefit by sharing information openly so that costs are minimized and both companies make good profits.

As is true in practically everything, there are truths to both positions. There are advantages and disadvantages to single sourcing and to multi-sourcing. If your volume is small, you simply lose negotiating power by dividing the pie. However, if your volume is very large, many suppliers may not have the capacity to meet all your requirements. Each case must be evaluated, and the pros and cons weighed.

Complete or Partial Product Purchase

Many companies prefer to do their own sourcing for each step in the manufacturing process. For example, if a casting needs to be heat treated, machined, and plated, the buyer would purchase each of these services separately. Other buyers encourage the primary supplier to subcontract the work. The primary supplier may or may not be completely in charge of coordinating the flow of work, making sure that all steps are completed on schedule so the final product is delivered when needed.

Either approach can cause problems, and the buyer must not underestimate his or her role in preventing or minimizing the problems with either method of buying.

If the primary source is allowed to subcontract various portions of the work, it is likely that additional costs will be incurred all along the way unless the buyer takes significant steps to avoid those extra costs. Most accountants will require markups on purchased goods to cover estimated or theoretical internal costs associated with those purchases. Thus, the total cost of the product will be higher than it would be if purchasing negotiated with each subcontractor.

However, if purchasing negotiates with each subcontractor, and any type of problem develops, such as delays in delivery, or less than satisfactory quality is involved, each supplier will try to pass the blame on to other suppliers in the chain. Pinpointing responsibility is often quite difficult, and the buyer is then left taking the heat for the failures. But it is not just accepting the blame that matters, it is trying to solve the problem that is important. When two or more suppliers are pointing fingers at each other, the problem does not get solved quickly.

Therefore, some purchasing managers would rather purchase an assembly or finished product from a given source and hold that source completely responsible to see that it is delivered satisfactorily. Even so, this method does not solve every situation because there will be a few suppliers who claim they cannot be responsible for the failures of their subcontractor. The buyer can avoid this situation by stressing orally and in writing the complete responsibility of the primary source. Then when any attempt to make excuses by blaming a subcontractor is given after an unsatisfactory performance, the buyer can and should be quick to place full responsibility on the primary source.

A similar problem revolves around the purchase of tooling. Fabricators may or may not make the tools they need to produce the products they sell. Tools such as patterns, dies, and molds are examples. If the fabricator does not produce these items, the buyer may decide to enter the picture by selecting the source who will make the tools, but the tool builder usually has to work closely with the fabricator so that the tools will match the equipment. When the buyer gets involved directly with the purchase of tooling from a separate company specializing in tool making, he or she either must have or obtain sufficient technical knowledge to avoid problems. For a further discussion of tooling issues, see Chapter 11.

Resolving Discrepancies and Problems

Every business has its share of problems and, of all departments, the purchasing function probably has more than its share. Solving those problems takes a significant amount of the buyer's time. Those problems and the time required to solve them can be minimized by good planning, proper policies and procedures, and good buying practices. Having well-educated and well-qualified buyers and purchasing management helps an organization keep problems at a minimum and makes solving the problems easier.

Difficulties surrounding purchasing activities can be divided into two major categories: those caused by internal factors, and those caused by the supplier. General management may be aware of one of these types, but may not be aware of both kinds of problems. However, if the causes are interpreted strictly, the supplier-related problems can be viewed as a result of poor internal performance; that is because the selection and management of suppliers is done by internal personnel.

Let us look at some of the most frequent and common problems faced by purchasing people and suggest some solutions.[2]

Problem 1 — Inappropriate Specifications: In most organizations, purchasing does not decide what to buy. The need is created by people in other departments, and either engineering or the user of the product describes what is desired.

If the specifications are insufficient to fully define the product, delivery of an inappropriate product often results. The product may be either needlessly expensive or insufficient to do the job the user wanted.

If the specifications are too restrictive or too detailed — usually by naming a particular brand or by providing a certain criteria that is only produced by one supplier — then purchasing is locked into that source and has no ability to negotiate. The result is usually a higher price than would otherwise be paid.

Solution: Make sure that engineering does not specify supplier names or brands. If the product is very complex and the engineering time required would be so great that it would be cost prohibitive to produce an adequate set of specifications, and brand names or supplier names must be used, then instruct engineers to add "or equivalent" after the named supplier or brand name.

A functional specification — describing what you want the product to do rather than the way it is to be built — is better than naming a supplier, brand name, or using the "or equivalent" statement.

Problem 2 — Backdoor Selling: It is the job of salespeople to get the order. They realize that in-house users can apply pressure to the authorized buyer to buy from them. Therefore, they make sales calls on nonpurchasing personnel to sell the user rather than the professional buyer. The user often has little sales resistance; is unfamiliar with negotiating techniques; and is susceptible to flattery, hype, and other selling techniques. Allowing such activity takes time away from the job the user is supposed to be doing, weakens the purchasing department's authority, and usually results in inferior products and higher costs.

Solution: Make it a rule that salespeople will always call on purchasing first before contacting any other employee in the organization — this means on every visit, not just the first. Encourage buyers to go with the salespeople if it is necessary to visit and discuss technical items with the users or engineers. Prohibit nonpurchasing employees from discussing prices or costs with suppliers; that should be reserved for the authorized buyer or purchasing analyst only.

Insist that only purchasing may give out purchase orders to suppliers. Do not permit purchasing personnel to give purchase order numbers to other employees to give to the suppliers.

Problem 3 — Failure to Meet Delivery Schedules: Additional costs are incurred when suppliers either ship earlier or later than scheduled by the order. Early shipments cause congestion on receiving docks and in storage areas. Late shipments disrupt production schedules resulting in inefficiency and added cost, and possibly may lead to delayed shipments to customers and to lost business.

Solution: Make sure that suppliers submit realistic lead times, rather than buyer-desired lead times in order to get the order. Write purchase orders to include a clause stating that "Time is of the essence." Stress the importance of meeting the promised delivery time schedule before the order is given to the supplier. Try to negotiate incentives for difficult delivery times and penalty clauses for late deliveries (be aware that penalty clauses may not be legally enforceable).

Ask each regularly used supplier to submit continual updated information on current normal lead time. Then have buyers periodically prepare an internal report for requestors and production control people and possibly the sales department showing such lead time. The internal lead time should include time for purchasing to process the requisition, time for the supplier to receive the order, time for the supplier to produce the item, and time for transportation of the material. The report should be sent to users and engineers who will submit purchase requests.

Problem 4 — Shortages or Excessive Inventory: Not infrequently, purchasing personnel or suppliers are blamed for out-of-stock conditions or even when there is too much inventory. The belief may be that purchasing did not place the order quickly enough, or that the buyer or purchasing manager did not put enough pressure on the supplier to deliver on time or to accept a cancellation of an order. Suppliers are blamed because they have long lead time or because they can't increase or decrease scheduled quantities. Pressure is exerted on the buyer to change suppliers.

Solution: While purchasing people and suppliers may not always be without blame, it is rare that they are the cause of the problem. Having enough inventory, but not more than needed, is a function of the service level that an organization desires. Keeping inventory to satisfy customers is a cost, and management must decide how much they are willing to invest and what percentage of time they want to have stock available. An infinite amount of inventory is required to fill every possible demand. Some companies are satisfied to have enough stock to fill orders 95% of the time. Others want to keep enough to meet demand 99% of the time. When the organization decides on the desired level, then good forecasts should be developed using modern statistical methods to predict requirements so that material can be ordered with sufficient lead time to meet schedules. The most efficient way to do this is by using the computer and a good statistical program.

Problem 5 — Dishonesty or Poor Ethical Practices: Every once in a while, the newspapers report how a buyer or business manager or government official has taken a "kickback" or received lavish entertainment in return for business. Probably more of this goes on than is reported, particularly in the private sector. When companies discover such problems, they tend to dismiss the employees involved and keep the event as quiet as possible.

Solution: Companies should have a written policy concerning ethical behavior of officers and employees. In addition, every purchasing department should have a written policy and procedure manual that clearly defines the ethical conduct expected of purchasing personnel.[3] Although public accounting firms periodically conduct audits of purchasing, the audits of purchasing are usually quite superficial. Internal audits or those done by a well-qualified purchasing consultant can be more thorough and effective. The recommendations made by those auditors should be carefully considered and implemented where practical.

Companies should investigate the backgrounds and reputations of candidates for buying and purchasing management positions before they are hired. Those buyers and managers who have earned certification through the American Purchasing Society have had their reputations checked by the Society before the certification was awarded.

Problem 6 — Late Payments to the Supplier: Every purchase obligates the buyer to pay for the goods or services in accordance with the terms of the agreement. If no terms have been discussed or written, payment is due upon delivery; but the most usual payment term is Net 30, or in 30 days after delivery. Buyers may negotiate earlier or later payment terms depending on other conditions of the order, and the company is obligated to pay in accordance with such negotiated terms agreed by both parties. Frequently, accounting people either fail to realize this obligation or unilaterally decide to ignore the agreements and delay payments. Their purpose is to improve cash flow or finance the purchase at the supplier's expense. This is a common practice. Although normal business payment terms are Net 30, average payment is made in about 45 days.

If the extra time taken is not excessively long, most suppliers will wait for the payments without saying anything to the buyer and the buyer may not even be aware of the late payments being made. Why risk embarrassing or offending the buyer and losing valuable business?

There are several things wrong with this practice. First, it weakens the buyer's position. Salespeople calling on the buyer no longer can believe that terms agreed upon with the buyer will be honored. Second, future prices, terms, and conditions will be adjusted to compensate for the longer terms.

Solution: If longer terms are desired, the buyer should negotiate for them and build them into the agreement. Terms of Net 60, Net 90, and longer are possible.

Problem 7 — Inability to Locate Qualified Suppliers: Inspectors constantly reject material from supplier after supplier. Internal production drops because of the inability to obtain satisfactory material.

Solution: There are several possible reasons, and the solution depends on the real cause of the problem. It could be that the quality demanded is impossible to produce; or it may be that the buyers have not looked everywhere for the best sources. More than likely the specifications are not clear or not in sufficient detail. Another possibility is that the evaluation of the product's quality is being carried out subjectively. There will be a continuing problem if the test of quality is arbitrary and by personal opinion only. The quality should be measurable and quantifiable.

Problem 8 — Costly Administrative Errors: Wrong part number, wrong prices, wrong quantities, wrong descriptions, or numerous other errors are typed on the purchase order. Incorrect invoices are received that don't match the purchase order. Packing slips don't match.

Solution: A high percentage of errors can be eliminated by using the computer. Once the information is entered into the computer correctly, it will feed back the same information correctly over and over again as many times as needed. Programming the computer with tests for accuracy will automatically rule out certain types of errors. For example, if quantities are normally ordered in hundreds, the computer can issue a warning or even lock out quantities that would be entered in thousands erroneously. A purchasing department not now computerized is working with a serious handicap.

Problem 9 — Poor Quality from Existing Suppliers: Material is now being received with poor quality from suppliers that were previously satisfactory.

Solution: You have to find out what else has changed. If only one supplier is at fault, the company may have changed management or processes. The buyer must be an investigator to find the cause. Perhaps specifications have been changed. Sometimes specifications or processes have been changed at the buying company, and products that worked before no longer work properly with the new processes or new equipment.

Problem 10 — Long Lead Time: Lead times are being extended and requestors are not allowing enough time to get material.

Solution: Make sure the suppliers are reporting changing lead times on a regular basis. Meet with the suppliers and find out why lead times are being lengthened. Visit the supplier's facilities to see if the causes can be determined. In one case, the supplier was having financial difficulties and could not afford to get raw material until more cash was received. In such a case, the buyer could purchase the material and have it delivered to the supplier for processing.

It may be necessary to increase inventory or buy from a second source in order to obtain enough material in time. Make sure that purchasing is reporting the extended lead time to the requestors or production control so they can adjust their planning.

Problem 11 — Delivery of Incorrect Counts: Quantity received is less than ordered and/or quantity received is less than billed.

Solution: Incorrect counts are usually innocent errors but should be infrequent. Continual errors or hidden discrepancies may point to something more sinister. First, make sure that the shortages are received that way by the receiving department and not reported within the plant, which could mean that the suppliers are not at fault. Find out if the packages were received intact and that the carrier was not to blame. Second, discuss the matter with the supplier and find out what steps the supplier will take to correct the situation. Suggest better scales, other personnel, inspectors, or other procedures to help the supplier improve.

Problem 12 — Receipt of Damaged Goods: There are two variations to the damaged goods problem: the package may look damaged when it is received, or the package is in good shape and there is no apparent damage.

Solution: The former scenario is easy to spot by a receiving clerk and may be refused or signed for on the carrier's papers, clearly indicating that the package or packages were damaged. The responsibility in resolving the problem technically depends on the F.O.B. terms or where title to the goods passed from buyer to seller. In practice, the buying company may file a claim with the carrier or ask the seller to do so. The carrier may deny that it caused the problem and say the goods were received in that fashion from the seller, but if the seller has the paperwork showing the goods were delivered to the carrier without the driver taking exception, it is likely that the carrier is responsible. If it is the buying company's material and must be paid for, the buyer should take prompt action and should not allow the problem to rest assuming it will be settled. Follow up with the seller or carrier or both until you are compensated.

Hidden damage is more difficult to settle because it is usually not discovered until long after the carrier has disappeared. The stock may already have been placed in storage, and days, weeks, or months have gone by before the shelf container is opened. The longer the time interval, the less likely there is to be compensation. One way to limit this type of occurrence is to spot check large shipments that are expected to be placed on the shelf for an extended period. Have a few of the boxes opened at random to check the contents. Most of the time, concealed or hidden damage is the fault of the supplier. At any rate, the buyer has a much better chance of being compensated by the supplier than the carrier. Even if the carrier is the primary suspect because the goods were carefully checked before shipment, their people will claim that the goods were not properly packaged or marked to protect them from damage from normal handling.

Problem 13 — Excessive Number of Suppliers: A company may have hundreds or even thousands of suppliers that it does business with. There may be two, three, or as many as a dozen suppliers for the same item or category of items. The problem with this is that it wastes time and is inefficient. It is costly in more than one respect. More time is spent discussing each transaction with each supplier. More shipments are received creating extra work for the receiving department and stock handlers. More invoices are received creating more work for accounting and requiring more checks to be issued. Using similar items from different suppliers can cloud responsibility for quality problems in a manufacturing environment.

Solution: As mentioned previously, there are advantages and disadvantages to having several sources for the same item. The trend in purchasing management has been to move from multisourcing to single sourcing. In order to do this successfully, the buyer must select a well-qualified supplier and build up a close relationship with the supplier. Intelligent purchasing requires an evaluation of the products, the market conditions, and the volume of the business. Certainly, spending a few dollars each with hundreds of suppliers provides little negotiating leverage. It is better to offer a few suppliers much more business to make it worthwhile for them to offer a better deal. Few will question that volume buyers pay less. It is up to purchasing management to insist that buyers keep the number of suppliers to a minimum.

Problem 14 — Insufficient Competition: Lack of competition for a product is always a difficult problem for buyers. There is a tendency to give up and just accept the situation. A supplier with a proprietary item, or a patented item, or with just a few ineffectual competitors, sometimes takes advantage of its good fortune. It may do this by pricing the product higher than reasonable, giving poor warranties, poor terms, long lead times, or poor service.

Solution: If you love a challenge, this is one to sink your teeth into. The buyer needs to use imagination and creativity. First of all, very few products have no substitute whatsoever. If you buy energy, it could be in the form of gas or oil. There are factories that have facilities to obtain heat or power from either material. They switch from oil to gas or gas to oil, depending on the price and availability of the product. You can substitute aluminum for steel or steel for aluminum. You can substitute a stamping for a forging or a casting for a weldment.

When a buyer negotiates with a supplier that thinks it has a monopoly or no serious competition, he or she should never let on that there is no substitute nor ever admit that there is no competition. The supplier may be 99% sure there is no competition, but there is always the element of doubt.

A buyer should begin looking for an alternate source the moment he or she is aware that there seems to be only one source. It is not unusual to find a substitute product that is better. It could be made in Europe or Asia or South America. Or it could be made in a small shop somewhere in the United States.

Engineers can design around patents. The buyer should make the problem known to company engineers and solicit their efforts in changing the design.

Another approach is to make an agreement with the existing supplier to continue buying for an extended period in return for better service, better prices, or whatever is needed, rather than change the design or use a substitute product.

Problem 15 — High Prices and Excessive Price Increases: One of the major functions of purchasing professionals is to keep costs at a minimum — and a major portion of total material costs is price. It is not an exaggeration to say that the profits or survival of a manufacturing company depend on what they pay for material and services. Yet not all companies in similar businesses pay the same amount for purchased goods and services. Conversely, one of the major functions of sales and marketing is to maximize profits and profits are at least in part a function of the price charged. Thus, salespeople are motivated to get what the market will bear. But some companies are more aggressive than others. They have a philosophy of charging top dollar and asking for increases whenever they think they will continue to receive orders. Paying excessive prices reduces or eliminates any profit the buying company might make.

Solution: Buyers must be aware of product cost. They must keep in close touch with the industries that supply the products they buy to know who the most competitive and uncompetitive producers are. They must continually shop and continually negotiate to obtain the lowest cost.

Once a buyer is satisfied that he or she is receiving a good low price for a commodity continually purchased, he or she should try to establish a long-term agreement at that price which allows for a price adjustment up or down because of documented cost changes only.

Buyers should always object to price increase announcements, especially blanket increases or industry-wide increases. Each item should be discussed separately and the component cost evaluated. Suppliers should support requests for price increases by documenting additional costs their own companies have incurred.

Problem 16 — Legal Violations or Lawsuits: Once in a while a buyer gets in trouble because he or she doesn't know anything about contract law or the antitrust laws or other aspects of the law that affect the purchasing operation. Legal problems can cost a company millions to resolve.

Solution: Managers should make sure that buyers have a minimum knowledge of the law. Have every buyer attend seminars regularly to keep up to date on new developments in the law. Encourage buyers to read periodicals, newsletters, or books that deal with the legal issues in purchasing.

Problem 17 — Unqualified Buyers or Excessive Purchasing Turnover: There is little doubt that a large percentage of buyers in industry are unqualified. The better buyers are often promoted or leave to go to another company. Too many companies have a revolving door for buyers and purchasing managers. Management is not satisfied with the job being done, but then goes out and hires someone who is no better. The big companies hire executive search firms to find well-qualified purchasing managers or purchasing vice presidents, but the firms they select to do the searches never hired a purchasing person before. The recruiters know nothing about buying. They interview the candidates, but don't know what to ask them. The candidates they eventually pass along to the company are interviewed by company managers who also know nothing about purchasing, and freely admit it. Often, the person selected is a manager who has been with the company a number of years and can be trusted. But he or she knows nothing about purchasing and has to learn on the job. It can take years — and plenty of mistakes — to learn. This is not an imaginary story. This has happened to many of the "Fortune 500" companies, and who knows how many companies of lesser size.

Solution: If you use outside search assistance, hire consultants who specialize in purchasing and who have had extensive experience in purchasing to search for qualified candidates. Avoid using accounting firms or well-recognized search firms that have little or no experience with purchasing. Obtain personnel with the proper credentials for the job. Managers and buyers should know contract law, be familiar with the principles of psychology, economics, and accounting. Managers should have knowledge of statistics, and know the principles of management. A knowledge of marketing is also helpful. Anyone entering purchasing— buyer or manager —should be able to do the required mathematics and have excellent communications skills. These skills are absolutely essential.

If you have a choice, choose the person who has been certified by the American Purchasing Society. The Society tests the above-mentioned skills and investigates the business reputation of each candidate before awarding certification.

Footnotes

[1] Adapted in part from an article in the January 1995 issue of *Professional Purchasing*, published by the American Purchasing Society, Inc., Port Richey, FL.

[2] For a more detailed discussion of these and other problems, see *Handbook of Buying and Purchasing Management* by Hough & Ashley, published by Prentice-Hall, Englewood Cliffs, NJ, 1992.

[3] The American Purchasing Society publishes a monthly written hard copy of a generic policy or procedure that is accompanied by a floppy disk that can be used to customize the material for any particular organization.

Glossary

ABS: A plastic copolymer material made from acrylonitrile, butadiene, and styrene.

alloy: A metal containing a certain minimum percentage of more than one element as a compound or mixture. In plastic, it is a product produced by combining two polymers.

alumina: Aluminum oxide produced from mined bauxite. It is a white powdery material that has the appearance of granulated sugar. It is an intermediate material in the production of aluminum from bauxite, but is also used for other purposes.

anneal or annealing: The process of heating various materials such as metal, glass, etc., to a temperature depending on the material, with the intended purpose of removing or preventing internal stress, and then slowly cooling the material. To temper.

anode: A positive electrode to which negative ions are attracted in an electrolytic cell. Also a rectangular plate of copper used in the electrolytic process.

anodizing: An electrochemical process for coating metal for the purpose of either protecting the metal or as a decoration.

APS: An abbreviation for the American Purchasing Society, a professional organization whose members are buyers, purchasing managers, and companies that purchase material for use in their business.

A.S.T.M.: An abbreviation for the American Society for Testing and Materials, an organization that develops and publishes standard specifications on many products.

bauxite: An ore that contains about 45% alumina.

Bessemer converter: A method of marking steel by directing a blast of air into molten pig iron and oxidizing carbon, manganese, phosphorus, and silicon.

billet: A semifinished shape of iron or steel that has been made from an ingot or bloom that has been rolled or hammered into the form of a cylinder or rectangle with a cross section 1.5 inches to 6 inches square (36 square inches).

bloom: A semifinished shape of metal having a cross section greater than 36 square inches.

blooming mill: The manufacturing plant devoted to producing blooms from ingots.

blow holes: A void or space in a metal as it cools and becomes a solid created by gas or air.

blow molding: A process of producing hollow plastic items such as bottles and other containers by blowing air under pressure into a cavity and forcing plastic material against a mold.

brazing: A process of flowing a thin layer of a molten alloy between other metal pieces to be joined.

Brinell hardness: A test of hardness by pressing a 1-centimeter ball into material and measuring the indentation. The area is divided into the load to give a number called a Brinell number and expressed in kilograms per square millimeter.

broaching: A machining process wherein a tool designed to give a particular shape is used to cut into stock and remove material to produce a finished product of the desired shape.

casting: The process of obtaining a desired shape of a metal product by pouring or forcing molten metal into a mold and letting it harden as it cools.

cathode: A negatively charged electrode. Cathode copper is a plate of pure metal produced by either electrolytic refining or another refining process.

certification: There are various types of certification. One is given by primary metal producers indicating the material has been tested. Another is an award referred to as ISO-9000, and is given to companies that meet certain quality standards. A third is the professional recognition given to individual buyers and purchasing managers by the American Purchasing Society.

cold shortness: A condition where metal lacks ductility or is brittle at low temperatures.

cold working: Bending, drawing, hammering, rolling, or application of other mechanical forces to a metal below the metal's recrystallization point and which results in hardening of the metal.

contract: An agreement between individuals or companies. For a contract to be legal, the parties involved must be capable in a legal sense, there must be an offer, there must be an acceptance, and there must be consideration (something given in return). A valid legal contract does not necessarily have to be in writing.

cope and drag: The top and bottom half of a mold. The cope is the upper half and the drag is the bottom.

CPP: Initials that are placed after a buyer or purchasing manager's name indicating that he or she has been awarded Certified Purchasing Professional status by the American Purchasing Society.

cupola: A type of furnace for melting iron for use in a foundry. Iron, coke, and flux are placed on top of coke and air is blown into the furnace.

dendrites: Crystals of a metal that have a structure resembling a tree.

die: A mold used in stamping, casting, or extruding that imparts the shape of the tool to the item being made.

drop forging: Shaping metal by using a machine that forces metal into dies. The upper die is hammered or dropped on the lower die to create the desired shape. This process is also called impact-die forging.

extractive metallurgy: It is also called process metallurgy and deals with how ores are mined and processed into metals.

flash: Extra material that extends around the die on a forging or casting that needs to be removed from the finished product.

flux: A material added to a furnace or used in the joining of other materials to remove oxides, or to lower the melting points of the other materials.

forging: A process of shaping metal material by hammering or applying force.

gangue: The waste material in an ore.

hot shortness: Steels that exhibit brittleness by tending to tear or crack during rolling processes. This is caused by the presence of more than twelve hundredths of a percent of sulfur in the form of iron sulfides. See cold shortness.

ingot: A semifinished solid metal casting ready for remelting or working.

ISO-9000: ISO stands for the International Organization for Standardization, which has 91 members, 9000 refers to the standard entitled, "Quality Management and Quality Assurance Standards: Guidelines for Selection and Use." The U.S. representative is the American National Standards Institute.

malleable casting: A type of iron casting that has been produced from what is called white cast iron that has been heat treated, making the metal capable of being shaped without breaking.

mill products: Metal that has been produced into a form that needs to be further processed in order to obtain a finished product.

monomers: A molecular structure unit in chemistry that combines with other similar or dissimilar units to form a polymer.

MRO: An abbreviation for Maintenance, Repair, and Operating supplies. It normally requires a different type of buying technique and management compared to production, raw material, and capital equipment purchasing. MRO items are usually purchased in low quantities and frequently are of relatively low value.

OEM: An abbreviation for Original Equipment Manufacturer. Suppliers usually give OEM customers, who purchase the products for ultimate resale, a lower price than those customers who use the products for internal use only.

open hearth furnace: A type of furnace used to make steel. Pig iron, scrap iron, and ore are melted in such a furnace using the heat from direct flame and from radiation from the sides and roof.

physical metallurgy: It is the branch of metallurgy that deals with the chemistry of metals, the mechanical treatment of metals, the manufacturing processing of metals, and how to use metals.

plastic deformation: Change in internal crystal structure of a metal or in the shape of a metal item by applying mechanical forces to the item.

polymer: A complex organic molecular material or plastic made up of monomers.

pot: The common name for an electrolytic reduction cell used to change alumina placed in molten cryolite into aluminum. A potline is a series of such cells that are connected electrically.

powder metallurgy: The study or process of using powdered metal to make a desired shape of a solid metal item by pressing, binding, and sintering.

resin: A natural or synthetic inorganic substance used to make plastic products.

Robinson–Patman: An antitrust law that makes it illegal to use unfair trading practices such as giving a supplier false information about what you are paying another supplier with the purpose of obtaining a lower price.

Rockwell hardness tester: A special machine to test the hardness of material by the amount of indentation which is indicated by a number that can be read out on a dial.

S.A.E: Abbreviation for the Society of Automotive Engineers, an organization that establishes its own set of material standards.

scratch hardness test: A quick and easy way to test hardness. A scratch is made on the material with a known pressure, and the width of the mark is measured, and thereby the resistance to the scratch is determined.

sintering: A process using heated, powdered metal or briquettes made of powdered metal to form solid items of a desired shape.

slip: A change in the shape or position of a crystal or where crystals or rows of atoms in a plane slide past each other and cause plastic deformation of the metal piece.

smelt: A process of melting ore to obtain or refine metal.

sprue: The opening used to pour or force the metal into a mold.

stamping: An item that is produced by any of various stamping or press processes such as blanking, shearing, drawing, bending, and coining. Most often, stampings are made out of sheet or coil steel.

swages: Various concave tools used to hammer metal to reduce its diameter.

swaging: Decreasing the diameter of the metal by using the forging process.

team buying: A method of buying which involves several people from the same organization working together to make purchases of the same item or items to obtain more suitable products and services. Usually the team consists of individuals from various departments such as engineering, quality control, production, and purchasing.

temper: A process whereby steel or cast iron is heated below the transformation point and then, after a period of time, is cooled at a controlled rate. The degree of hardness and strength as a result of such a process or by cold working of the metal. Also the percentage of carbon in tool steel.

the work: The piece of metal being forged.

thermoplastic: A substance that becomes soft each time it is heated and hard each time it is cooled. Typical examples include acrylics, cellulosics, nylons, and vinyls.

Uniform Commercial Code: Commonly referred to as the UCC. A document proposed as law by the American Bar Association to all states to make the interpretation of business transactions easier or more similar. Now accepted with minor variations by all states, except Louisiana, the law requires that all transactions for goods of $500 or more must be in some written form to be enforceable.

upsetting: Decreasing the length and increasing the diameter using the forging process.

value: The material for which an ore is mined. Also the worth of something.

weldment: An assembly of components welded together such as a steel metal table or base for a machine tool.

work hardening: The hardening of a material as a result of mechanical, physical forces such as hammering, rolling, etc. See **cold working**.

Selected Bibliography

Books

Accounting and Finance

Dixon, Robert L. *The McGraw-Hill 36-Hour Accounting Course,* Second Edition, New York, NY: McGraw-Hill Book Company, 1982.

Spurga, Ronald C. *Balance Sheet Basics, Financial Management for Nonfinancial Managers,* New York, NY: MENTOR, published by Penguin Group, 1987.

Law

Ambrose, Cunningham, Hancock, Rolitsky, and Victor. *Legal Aspects of International Sourcing,* Chesterland, OH: Business Laws, Inc., 1986.

Ellentuck, Elmer, Ed. *Purchasing and the Law, A Handbook of Cases for Purchasing Managers,* New York, NY: BRP Publications, Inc., 1992.

General Information Concerning Patents, Washington, DC: U.S. Department of Commerce, 1989.

Hancock, W. A. *The Law of Purchasing,* Chesterland, OH: Business Laws, Inc., 1982.

Prentice-Hall Editorial Staff. *Lawyer's Desk Book,* Ninth Edition, Englewood Cliffs, NJ: Prentice-Hall, Inc., 1989.

Ritterskamp, Jr. *Purchasing Manager's Desk Book of Purchasing Law*, Englewood Cliffs, NJ: Prentice-Hall, Inc., 1987.

Ritterskamp, Jr. *1990 Supplement, Purchasing Manager's Desk Book of Purchasing Law*, Englewood Cliffs, NJ: Prentice-Hall, Inc., 1990.

Stone, Bradford. *Uniform Commercial Code in a Nut Shell*, St. Paul, MN: West Publishing Co., 1975.

Materials Management

Ammer, Dean S. *Materials Management and Purchasing*, Fourth edition, Homewood, IL: Richard D. Irwin, Inc., 1980.

Hall, Robert W. with American Production & Inventory Control Society. *Zero Inventories*, Homewood, IL: Dow Jones-Irwin, 1983.

Janson, Robert L. *Handbook of Inventory Management*, Englewood Cliffs, NJ: Prentice-Hall, Inc., 1987.

Mather, Hal. *How To Really Manage Inventories*, New York, NY: McGraw-Hill Book Company, 1984.

Orlicky, Joseph. *Materials Requirements Planning*, New York, NY: McGraw-Hill Book Company, 1975.

Manufacturing Processes

Brown, James. *Modern Manufacturing Processes*, New York, NY: Industrial Press Inc., 1991.

Dietert, Harry W. *Foundry Core Practice*, Third edition, Des Plaines, IL: American Foundrymen's Society, 1966.

Investment Casting Handbook, Investment Casting Institute, 1979.

Jenson, Jon E. *Forging Industry Handbook*, Cleveland, OH: Forging Industry Association, 1966.

Little, Richard L. *Metalworking Technology*, New York, NY: McGraw-Hill Book Company, 1977.

Machinery's Handbook, 25th Edition, New York, NY: Industrial Press Inc., 1996.

Schey, John A. *Introduction to Manufacturing Processes*, New York, NY: McGraw-Hill Book Company, 1977.

Selected ASTM Standards for the Purchasing Community, Second Edition, Philadelphia, PA: ASTM, 1990.

Todd, Robert H.; Allen, Dell K.; and Alting, Leo. *Fundamental Principles of Manufacturing Processes*, New York, NY: Industrial Press Inc., 1994.

Todd, Robert H.; Allen, Dell K.; and Alting, Leo. *Manufacturing Processes Reference Guide*, New York, NY: Industrial Press Inc., 1994.

Wright, R. Thomas. *Processes of Manufacturing*, South Holland, IL: The Goodheart-Willcox Company, Inc., 1987.

Negotiating

Fisher, Roger and Ury, William. *Getting To Yes, Negotiating Agreement Without Giving In*, Boston, MA: Houghton Mifflin Company, 1981; New York, NY: Penguin Books, 1983 (Paperback).

Fisher, Roger and Brown, Scott. *Getting Together, Building Relationships As We Negotiate*, Boston, MA: Houghton Mifflin Company, 1988; New York, NY: Penguin Books, 1989 (Paperback).

Cohen, Herb. *You Can Negotiate Anything*, Secaucus, NJ: Lyle Stuart Inc., 1980.

Fuller, George. *The Negotiator's Handbook*, Englewood Cliffs, NJ: Prentice-Hall, Inc., 1991.

Karrass, Chester L. *Give & Take, The Complete Guide to Negotiating Strategies and Tactics*, New York, NY: Thomas Y. Crowell Company, 1974.

Kellar, Robert E. *Sales Negotiating Handbook*, Englewood Cliffs, NJ: Prentice-Hall, Inc., 1988.

Koch, H. William, Jr. *Negotiator's Factomatic*, Englewood Cliffs, NJ: Prentice-Hall, Inc., 1988.

Leritz, Len. *No-Fault Negotiating*, New York, NY: Warner Books, Inc., 1987.

Mastenbroek, William, *Negotiate*, First translation, Oxford and New York, NY: Basil Blackwell Inc., 1989.

Nierenberg, Gerard I. *Fundamentals of Negotiating*, New York, NY: Harper & Row Publishers, Inc., 1973. Available in paperback from Perennial Library Division of Harper & Row.

Raiffa, Howard. *The Art & Science of Negotiation*, Cambridge, MA, and London, England: The Belknap Press of Harvard University Press, 1982.

Rubin, Jeffrey Z. and Brown, Bert R. *The Social Psychology of Bargaining and Negotiation*, New York, NY: Academic Press, Subsidiary of Harcourt Brace Jovanovich Publishers, 1975.

Schatzki, Michael with Coffey, Wayne R. *Negotiation, The Art of Getting What You Want*, New York, NY: Signet, The New American Library, Inc., 1981.

Warschaw, Tessa Albert. *Winning By Negotiation*, New York, NY: McGraw-Hill Paperbacks, 1980.

Prices and Costs

Brown, James. *Value Engineering*, New York, NY: Industrial Press, 1992.

Armed Services Pricing Manual, 2 volumes, Chicago, IL: Commerce Clearing House, Inc., 1987.

Figgie, Harry E. Jr. *Cutting Costs, An Executive's Guide to Increased Profits*, Paperback edition, New York, NY: AMACOM Division, American Management Association, 1990.

Purchasing, General

Burt, David N. *Proactive Procurement, The Key To Increased Profits, Productivity, and Quality*, Englewood Cliffs, NJ: Prentice-Hall, Inc., 1984.

Corey, E. Raymond. *Procurement Management: Strategy, Organization, and Decision-Making*, Boston, MA: CBI Publishing Company, Inc., 1976.

Federal Acquisition Regulation, Chicago, IL: Commerce Clearing House, Inc., 1987.

Harding, Michael. *Profitable Purchasing*, New York, NY: Industrial Press, 1990.

Heinritz, Farrell, Giunipero, and Kolchin. *Purchasing Principles and Applications*, Eighth Edition, Englewood Cliffs, NJ: Prentice-Hall, Inc., 1991.

Hough, Harry E. and Ashley, James M. *Handbook of Buying and Purchasing Management*, Englewood Cliffs, NJ: Prentice-Hall, Inc., 1992.

Woodside, Arch G. and Vyas Nyren. *Industrial Purchasing Strategies*, Lexington, MA: Lexington Books Division of D. C. Heath and Company, 1987.

Leenders, Fearon, and England. *Purchasing and Materials Management*, Ninth Edition, Homewood, IL: Richard D. Irwin, Inc., 1989.

Professional Purchasing Study Material and Certification Guidance Manual, Port Richey, FL: American Purchasing Society, 1990.

Scheuing, Eberhard E. *Purchasing Management*, Englewood Cliffs, NJ: Prentice-Hall, Inc., 1989.

Quality

Barra, Ralph. *Putting Quality Circles To Work*, New York, NY: McGraw-Hill Book Company, 1983.

Crosby, Philip B. *Quality Is Free, The Art of Making Quality Certain*, New York, NY: McGraw-Hill Book Company, 1979.

Fernandez, Rick. *Total Quality in Purchasing and Supplier Management*, Delray Beach, FL: St. Lucie Press Corporation, 1994.

Ingle, Sud. *In Search of Perfection, How to Create/Maintain, Improve Quality*, Englewood Cliffs, NJ: Prentice-Hall, Inc., 1985.

Mauch, Stewart, and Straka. *The 90-Day ISO Manual*, Delray Beach, FL: St. Lucie Press Corporation, 1994.

Omachonu and Ross. *Principles of Total Quality*, Delray Beach, FL: St. Lucie Press Corporation, 1994.

Voehl, Jackson, and Ashton. *ISO 9000: An Implementation Guide for Small to Mid-Sized Business*, Delray Beach, FL: St. Lucie Press Corporation, 1994.

Periodicals

Ceramic Industry, published monthly except in July when two issues are published, by Business News Publishing Co., 775 W. Big Beaver Road, Suite 1000, Troy, MI, 48084-4900. Information and news about refractories, traditional and advanced ceramic manufacturing.

Electronic Buyers' News, newsweekly for the electronics industry with information about suppliers to the electronic industry and buyers of electronic components. Manhasset, NY: CMP Publications, Inc.

Foundry Management & Technology, published monthly for the casting industry by Penton Publishing, Inc., Cleveland, OH.

Iron Age, published monthly for the primary metals industry by Capital Cities Media, Inc., New York, NY.

Professional Purchasing, newsletter providing information on how to buy and manage purchasing. Port Richey, FL: American Purchasing Society, Published monthly. Free to members of the Society.

Purchasing magazine covers a wide variety of purchasing and purchasing related subjects. Newton, MA: Cahners Publishing Company. Semimonthly.

Cassettes

Crosby, Philip B. *Quality Is Free, The Art of Making Quality Certain*, Fullerton, CA: McGraw-Hill, 1989.

Crosby, Philip B. *Quality Without Tears, The Art of Hassle-Free Management*, Fullerton, CA: McGraw-Hill, 1989.

Fisher, Roger and Ury, William. *Getting To Yes, How To Negotiate Agreement Without Giving In*, Six Audiocassettes and a study guide, New York, NY: Simon & Schuster Audio Publishing Division, 1986.

Hough, Harry E. *Negotiating for Purchasing*, Port Richey, FL: American Purchasing Society, 1991.

Dawson, Roger. *The Secrets of Power Negotiating*, Chicago, IL: Nightingale-Conant Corporation, 1990.

Hough, Harry E. *Purchasing and Accounting, Transactions Between The Departments*, Port Richey, FL: American Purchasing Society, 1991.

Hough, Harry E. *Purchasing and Engineering*, Port Richey, FL: American Purchasing Society, 1991.

Nierenberg, Gerard I. *The Art of Negotiation*, Holmes, PA: Sound Editions from Random House, 1987.

Reck, Ross R. and Long, Brian G. *The Win Win Negotiator*, Chicago, IL: Nightingale-Conant Corporation, 1985.

Warschaw, Tessa Albert. *Negotiating To Win*, Fullerton, CA: TDM/McGraw-Hill, 1987.

Appendix I

Weight: Avoirdupois Equivalents

1 dram = 1.772 grams

1 ounce = 28.3495 grams

1 pound = 453.59 grams

1 short ton = 2000 pounds

1 gross or long ton = 2240 pounds

1 short ton = 907.18 kilograms or 0.9072 metric tons

1 long ton = 1,016.05 kilograms or 1.0160 metric tons

1 troy ounce = 31.1035 grams

1 troy pound = 373.24 grams

Linear Measure

1 inch = 2.54 centimeters

1 foot = 0.3048 meters

1 yard = 0.9144 meters

1 cubic inch = 16.387 cubic centimeters

1 cubic foot = 0.0283 cubic meters

1 cubic yard = 0.7646 cubic meters

Square Measure

1 base box = 31,360 square inches or 217.78 square feet

1 base box = 112 sheets measuring 14 X 20 inches

1 SITA = 100 square meters (SITA stands for System International
   Tinplate Area)

How to Convert Units of Measure

Inches to centimeters	Multiply number of inches by 2.54
Inches to millimeters	Multiply number of inches by 25.4
Fahrenheit to centigrade, Celsius, or kelvin	Subtract 32 from the number of degrees Fahrenheit and multiply the result by 0.556.
Centigrade to Fahrenheit	Multiply the number of degrees centi grade by 1.8 and add 32 to the result.

Appendix II

Supplier Directories

The following are names of directories that help locate sources of supply. The samples given in this book provide a start if you are shopping for the products described. For a more extensive and comprehensive shopping effort, use these directories.

General Product Directories

MacRae's Blue Book: A listing of 50,000 manufacturers. Company and trade name are indexed as well as manufacturers by product. Price is $165 and it is available from MacRae's Blue Book Inc., 65 Bleecker Street, 5th Floor, New York, NY 10012, FAX 212 475-1790.

Thomas Register of American Manufacturers: *Thomas Register* consists of 23 volumes. It includes names and addresses of manufacturers and the products and services they offer. The biggest drawback to the *Thomas Register* is that it does not give the names of sales personnel of the companies that are listed. Neither does it give much financial data. The total cost of all volumes is $240, and they may be ordered from the Circulation Department, Thomas Register, Thomas Publishing Company, One Penn Plaza, New York, NY 10117-0138.

Directory of Metal Suppliers: A supplement to *Purchasing Magazine* published by Cahners Publishing Co., 275 Washington St., Newton, MA 02158-1630.

Finding International Sources

There may be as many international directories as there are domestic directories. Listed below are a few. If you cannot locate a directory for the country you are interested in, contact the Consulate for that country. Offices are in Washington, but many also have offices in other major cities. The Consul will see which companies are interested in exporting to the U.S. or will give you a list of companies that you can contact directly.

Directory of Hong Kong Industries: Includes advertisements, list of products and the Hong Kong companies that sell them. Description of companies is given with some providing names of key executives. For further information contact the Management & Industrial Consultancy Div., Hong Kong Productivity Council, 12/F., World Commerce Centre, Harbour City, Kowloon, Hong Kong.

Italian Yellow Pages for the U.S.A.: Contains Italian companies and the products they sell. Published by SEAT — Societa Elenchi Ufficiali Abbonati al Telefono — a cooperative effort of AT&T, ItalCable, and SEAT. Contact AT&T International Business Markets Group, 412 Mt. Kemble Avenue, Morristown, NJ 07960.

Irish Export Directory : Lists companies and products. Published on behalf of Coras Trachtala/Irish Export Board by Jemma Publication, Ltd. 22 Brookfield Avenue, Blackrock Co, Dublin, Ireland.

Japan Yellow Pages: Contains Japanese companies and the products they sell. To order or for price information, contact Japan Yellow Pages Ltd., ST Bldg., 6-9 Iidabashi 4-chome, Chiyoda-ku, Tokyo 102, Japan.

Made in Europe, Monthly Import Guide and Continuous Trade Fair in Print: Includes advertisements for products produced in Europe. Published by Made in Europe Marketing Organization GmbH & Co. KG, 21-29 Unterlindau, D-6000 Frankfurt am Main 1, West Germany.

Taiwan Hardware Buyers' Guide: Includes advertisements, articles, and a list of companies and what they sell. Published by Trade Winds, Inc., P.O. Box 7-179, Taipei 10602, Taiwan, R.O.C.

Trade Associations

Look up the name of the appropriate association in National Trade and Professional Associations of the United States, which is available in most libraries, or purchase it for $55 from Columbia Books, Inc. 1212 New York Avenue, N.W., Suite 330, Washington, DC 20005.

Index